THE MEDEDITS GUIDE TO
MEDICAL SCHOOL
ADMISSIONS

ACRONYMS

This book uses many acronyms, including the following:

AACOMAS®: American Association of Colleges of Osteopathic Medicine Application Service

AAMC: Association of American Medical Colleges

AMCAS®: American Medical College Application Service

AO: All other (refers to GPA)

BCPM: Biology, chemistry, physics, math (refers to GPA)

COMLEX®: Comprehensive Osteopathic Medical Licensing Exam

CV: Curriculum Vitae

DO: Doctor of Osteopathy

FAFSA®: Free Application for Federal Student Aid

FAP: Fee Assistance Program

GPA: Grade point average

MCAT®: Medical College Admission Test

MD: Doctor of Medicine

MMI: Multiple Mini Interview

MPH: Master of Public Health

NRMP®: National Residency Matching Program

PBL: Problem based learning

PhD: Doctor of Philosophy

TMDSAS®: Texas Medical & Dental Application Service

USMLE®: United States Medical Licensing Exam

ALSO BY DR. JESSICA FREEDMAN

The Medical School Interview

How To Be an All-Star Residency Match Applicant

Dr. Freedman is the founder and president of
MedEdits Medical Admissions (www.mededits.com)

TABLE OF CONTENTS

PART 1

SO YOU WANT TO GO TO MEDICAL SCHOOL!

INTRODUCTION

As a former medical school and residency admissions officer and faculty member, I became well versed in how applications are reviewed and evaluated. Since leaving the Mount Sinai School of Medicine faculty, I have been working privately with clients applying to medical school, residency, and fellowship. My work with MedEdits has given me an even greater understanding of the process because now I not only have an idea of what happens on the "inside," but I also understand the misconceptions that applicants have, the mistakes they make, and how an applicant's approach to the medical school admissions process can influence success. I work with a wide spectrum of applicants. Some of our students aim for admissions to extremely competitive medical schools in the United States while others hope to get into a top off-shore or osteopathic medical school. These combined perspectives, and my own effort to stay educated and informed about developments and advances in medical education and admissions, allow me to write about what applicants and their parents need to know to be well prepared for the medical school admissions process.

Finding numerous sources for advice in the medical school admissions process is easy. In fact, most people, including parents, cousins, friends, and even your next door neighbor who is a second year medical school student, may be eager to offer their two cents about what you should do to get into medical school. However, only someone who has actually worked for an extended time on a medical school faculty and who understands what goes on behind the scenes in a medical school admissions office can offer a nuanced understanding of what it takes to get into medical school. Premedical advisors are often underinformed and overwhelmed, and every year I have applicants who call me for help because their premed advisors' advice didn't really make sense. There is no formal training for becoming an undergraduate premed advisor and while some advisors offer excellent guidance, many can offer only the advice that was "passed down" to them by their predecessor.

For example, I worked with an applicant whose premed advisor told him that since his grade point average at a top tier undergraduate college was "only" 3.6 he had no chance of being admitted to a "top" medical school. This applicant also worked full time as an undergraduate to support himself financially, had done impressive research, founded a not-for-profit organization, and had excellent clinical exposure. The applicant was also humble, compassionate, and sensitive and possessed many qualities and characteristics that medical schools are seeking. After working with this applicant to develop excellent written documents that clearly explained how his challenges helped nurture his character and interest in medicine, and helping him feel comfortable expressing his challenges during interviews, he was accepted to those very schools that his premed advisor told him were impossible.

Another applicant, also a top tier liberal arts college graduate, was advised that with a grade point average of 3.56, an MCAT® of 30, and few medically related experiences, she should apply only to top tier medical schools because of the undergraduate school's excellent reputation. This applicant was not successful on her first medical school application attempt and was accepted to medical school only once she reapplied to medical schools that were not so competitive.

I also remember a student who attended a competitive undergraduate institution who had a good, but not stellar, GPA. The student's premedical committee refused to write this student a committee letter in support of her candidacy. We worked "behind the scenes" with this student to help her advocate for herself. Not only did she ultimately convince the committee to write her a letter, but this student was accepted to several US allopathic medical schools on the first attempt.

The premed advisors with whom these applicants worked were not malicious, but they most likely were overwhelmed with large numbers of students, not familiar with the medical school admissions process, or did not fully understand what admissions committees are seeking. The premed advisors also might not have had enough time to really get to know these applicants on more than a superficial level, which limited the advice they could offer. Helping an applicant put together a quality application requires more than simply glancing at a resume; the best advisors help applicants by working one on one with each of them, taking the time to know who each applicant is and what motivates him or her.

Many people misunderstand the role of a private admissions consultant. I see my role as an extension of the work I enjoyed most when I worked in formal academic medicine, namely advising students and medical trainees. As a private advisor, I do not make "behind the scenes" phone calls or "pull strings" but instead help applicants market themselves effectively by learning about their interests in medicine and what motivates this interest. I also learn about applicants' backgrounds, challenges, hobbies, and interests to advise them how best to use this information. Most premedical advisors, simply put, do not have the time to offer this personalized attention. It is also important that applicants compose their own documents; most skilled admissions officers can sniff out ghost writers, especially if the way an applicant speaks during the interview doesn't "match" his or her voice on paper.

As you read this book, think about who you are, what led you to consider a career in medicine, and how you are going to show that you possess the academic aptitude and the personal qualities and characteristics that will make you a great doctor. Even though the competition to get into medical school is fierce, if you are committed, hardworking, and smart, you can get there. This book covers a wide range of topics, from what prerequisites you need for medical school admission to how you should write a letter of intent if you are waitlisted at your first choice school. Whether you are a high school student considering a career in medicine, a parent who is seeking information to help guide your child, or an applicant sitting down to compose an application, this book will help you understand what it takes to apply to medical school. This book is primarily intended for those applying to allopathic medical schools in the United States via the American Medical Colleges Application Service (AMCAS®), but applicants to Texas, osteopathic, and off-shore medical schools also will find chapters dedicated to those schools and useful advice.

Since about 50% of applicants to medical school are now "non-traditional" and take at least one "gap year" between college and medical school, the book focuses on topics that are important for all applicants, regardless of their path to medicine. I have tried to make the flow of the book logical; how important a particular topic is to you will depend on where you are in the process.

Some of the examples of personal statements, application entries, secondary essays, and letters of intent in this book are written by some of the applicants with whom I have worked and some by applicants with whom I did not work. Do not copy or plagiarize any information in this book. All information is intended for educational purposes only; the information in this book will in no way guarantee an applicant's success in the medical school admissions process.

The competition

In 2014, there were nearly 50,000 applicants to allopathic medical schools in the United States. About 37,000 were first time applicants. Slightly more than 20,000 students, actually matriculated, however. Needless to say, with fewer than half of applicants accepted, the competition is fierce. At the same time, the credentials of applicants who are accepted represent a tremendous range, as do those who are not accepted. For example, even some applicants with impressively high Medical College Admissions Test® (MCAT®) scores and grade point averages (GPAs) are not accepted. Indeed, the Association of American Medical Colleges® (AAMC) aggregate data from 2011 to 2013 show that 8.4% of applicants with GPAs of 3.8 to 4.0 and MCAT® scores between 39 and 45 were not accepted to medical school. So even applicants with the best "stats" are not guaranteed admission to medical school. And even those with an impressive GPA and MCAT® scores need to remain humble throughout the medical school admissions process. With medical school admissions committees focusing more on applicants' interpersonal qualities and characteristics, no score or GPA ever guarantees admission.

So what is most important in getting into medical school?

Despite the caveats I have noted about grades and scores, the single most important factor in determining whether or not you are accepted to medical school is academic performance. This includes GPA and MCAT® scores. Many medical schools screen applications based on average academic statistics, making no allowance for undergraduate institutions' being prestigious and notoriously difficult. This is something premed students should keep in mind in choosing where to attend college (see "Does it matter where I go to college?"). I often work with applicants who say, "But my college is so tough. Won't the admissions committee take that into account and give me a break?" The answer is "maybe." If your numbers are within screening "cut-offs," the medical school will take the competitiveness of your college into consideration but if not, the medical school will never even review your file. Even though it is never clearly advertised or stated, many medical schools do "screen" applications based on data such as GPA and/or MCAT® scores. These screening cut-offs vary from school to school. For example, one school might disregard applications with an overall GPA of lower than a 3.5 while another might use an MCAT® cut-off. Another school might use a cut-off that combines GPA and MCAT®.

What is the average GPA and MCAT® of medical school matriculants?

In 2014, the average metrics for US allopathic medical school matriculants was as follows:

1. MCAT®: 31.4 (VR: 10, PS: 10.6, BS: 10.9)
2. GPA Science: 3.63
3. GPA Non-Science: 3.77
4. GPA Total: 3.69

In 2013, the average metrics for US osteopathic medical school matriculants was as follows:

5. MCAT®: 26.87 (VR: 8.72, PS:8.74, BS: 9.41)
6. GPA Science: 3.38
7. GPA Non-Science: 3.60
8. GPA Total: 3.5

Does it matter where I go to college?

Going to the "best college" to which you are accepted may not always be a wise choice if you are certain that you want to go to medical school. If a college is notorious for "weeder" premedical classes or is known to have impossible curves, your GPA may suffer by attending such an undergraduate institution and negatively influence your chance of admission to medical school. I do advise all students to attend four year universities rather than community colleges if they plan to apply to medical school since community college classes are not considered as rigorous and most admissions committees do not respect grades from community college courses. As you decide where to attend college, also consider class sizes. A common applicant complaint is, "But my classes are huge. My professors don't know me and I have no one I can ask for letters of reference." In other words, if you know you want to go to medical school, consider the academic competitiveness of the school and class sizes in making your college choice.

What may be best is to attend a reputable undergraduate college—but one that is not notorious for making it very tough to earn good grades—where you will get a solid educational foundation in the sciences and where you will have the chance to work directly with your professors rather than teaching assistants. As you make your college choice, seek out information on how premedical students fare. Ask college administrators the following questions:

What percentage of students who enter college as "premeds" graduate and attend medical school?

Where do graduates attend medical school?

What percentage of students who want to apply to medical school are "approved" for a premedical committee letter (see more information on the premedical committee letter in Chapter 5).

Most important, however, is to attend a college where you can pursue your intellectual curiosities. Medical school admissions committees do not require applicants to major in a science (but you will need to enroll in challenging science courses). In fact, with medical schools seeking diverse student bodies, admissions committees like to see distinctive and atypical majors. Medical school admissions officers like applicants with academic diversity; consider a major or minor in a nonscience discipline such as art history or Hispanic studies, for example. Your intellectual pursuits during college can actually distinguish you during the application process. While you are in college might also be one of the last times you can pursue your nonmedical and scientific interests in depth so make the most of it!

PART 2

PREMEDICAL CONCERNS

CHAPTER 1

ACADEMICS

Even if you have outstanding extracurricular accomplishments, if you don't have "the numbers" to get in, your application may never be reviewed (see "What is holistic review?").

Once again, academic excellence is the key ingredient to gain admission to medical school. You will see this theme repeated throughout the book.

What is holistic review?

Medical school admissions committees now emphasize the importance of holistic review. This means considering the whole applicant and broadening what admissions committees consider when deciding whom to offer interviews, acceptances, and rejections. This holistic approach encourages admissions committees to look "beyond the numbers" of MCATs® and GPAs. Every applicant pool includes people with high MCATs® and GPAs who don't have the ideal personal attributes for practicing medicine, while other applicants in the pool with less than stellar "numbers" will make wonderful doctors. Medical schools are seeking applicants with the personal qualities and characteristics that make great doctors and want their students to represent a broad range of experiences, interests, and backgrounds, none of which is necessarily reflected by GPAs and MCAT® scores. With holistic review, applicants are reviewed in a more individualized way that considers each person's academic metrics, experiences, and personal qualities and characteristics.

Schools vary in the type of holistic review they practice, however. For example, a school based in an inner city that wants to nurture physicians who will care for those types of populations in the future might be looking specifically for experiences demonstrating work with similar populations and an understanding of those populations. By the same token, a school that values rural medicine might look for applicants with that type of experience. A research-focused school, on the other hand, will pay special attention to the research an applicant has done. In other words, in evaluating applicants holistically, medical schools want to ensure that the applicant is aligned with the school's mission and ideals.

Nonetheless, not all medical schools are practicing holistic review in deciding whom to interview and accept. These schools may miss some stellar applicants, but there are practical reasons why they don't embrace this process. First of all, medical schools simply don't have enough "people power" to review each and every application by hand, as holistic review demands. Second, given the sheer number of applications medical schools receive, they are under considerable pressure to have cut-offs for grades and MCAT® scores. Fortunately, some outstanding and highly competitive medical schools nonetheless have the luxury of choice; even if they have "high cut-offs" for MCATs® and GPAs, they still have a large enough pool of viable applicants to choose those with both "great numbers" and outstanding personal attributes.

Prerequisites

Certain core prerequisites are required for medical school admission; these courses also include the some of the primary content that is tested on the MCAT2015® (see "What are medical school prerequisites?"). With the MCAT2015, students will still have to take courses that are prerequisites for medical school. However, the MCAT2015® also requires—and tests—some subjects that are not prerequisites at all medical schools. In addition to expecting you to take certain prerequisites, medical schools also like students to enroll in upper level science and mathematics courses such as immunology, statistics, and computer science. Why? As a physician you will be expected to practice evidence-based medicine, which requires an understanding of how to critically evaluate studies in the medical literature. Some medical schools also require that students take English, genetics, and humanities courses.

What are medical school prerequisites?

Introductory Biology (two semester sequence)
Inorganic (general) chemistry (two semester sequence)
Organic chemistry (two semester sequence)

Physics (two semester sequence)
English (some medical schools require)
Calculus and/or college mathematics (some medical schools require)

The following courses are additional prerequisites for the MCAT2015®. At the time this book was written, all medical schools did not require the prerequisite MCAT2015® courses for admission to medical school however.

Biochemistry (first semester)
Introductory sociology (one semester)
Introductory psychology (one semester)

Check with your premed advisor to find out exactly what courses your college recommends. Some medical schools have specific prerequisites so always check what prerequisites are required at each medical school you are considering.

What about advanced placement (AP) credit?

Many students who take AP classes in high school "place out" of some required prerequisites in college. Not all medical schools will accept this AP credit, however, so it is important to check with individual medical schools regarding specific requirements. I suggest that students seek out this information before starting their freshman year. For example, I have worked with clients who "placed out of biology" and took chemistry their freshman year and organic chemistry and biochemistry during the sophomore year. Not only was their sophomore year course load very demanding, but once they realized that some medical schools would not accept their AP biology credit, they had to "go back" and take general college biology as a junior.

In what should I major?

Applicants often ask me what major "looks good" on an application. My response is always, "the one that interests you the most." Students can major in nonscience disciplines. In fact, medical schools are always seeking applicants who are intellectually curious and diverse; they don't want an entire class of biology and chemistry majors. If you do choose to major in a nonscience, however, consider taking some upper division science classes to prove that you can perform well in them, something medical schools like to see whatever an applicant's major. Independent research, whether for credit or during a summer break, is also looked upon favorably. Medical schools like to know that you have the ability to think critically, design an experiment or project to study a topic or answer a question, evaluate and interpret data, and understand its significance. Though this kind of research traditionally is associated with a scientific discipline, you will learn these same skills by doing research in other disciplines, including the humanities, economics, and math. Therefore, high level research in other disciplines is also respected and valued.

CHAPTER 2

GRADE POINT AVERAGES

Everyone knows that a high GPA is an extremely significant factor in gaining admission to medical school. But it is important to realize that medical school admissions committees see more than your overall GPA; on your application they view your grades in a three-part grid for each year of your education and are able to see all your science courses at a glance, allowing them to review the name of each course in which you have enrolled and the grade you earned in it. This is why all applicants must be able to explain not just an overall poor performance but why their performance was "off" in a specific class. On interviews (more about this below), be prepared to explain why you received anything lower than a B (or 3.0) in any course on your transcript. You must also be able to explain any "outliers." For example, if you earned all As (or 4.0s), even one B+ (or 3.3) will jump off the page.

The GPA grid

BCPM
The first column in the GPA grid is the "BCPM" column. BCPM stands for biology, chemistry, physics, and math

(see "Which courses does BCPM include?"). In other words, the first column includes all of your science and mathematics classes and is listed first because medical schools consider these classes most important. If you do not know how some of your classes are classified, check the AMCAS® instructions or check with your registrar.

AO
The next column in the grid is "AO" or all other. This grid includes all courses that are not considered "BCPM."

Total
The final column in the grid is "Total," which is your total GPA combined.

Which courses does BCPM include?

If you have taken an esoteric course that is not listed below, contact your registrar to find out how it should be listed.

Biology:

Anatomy	Biology
Biophysics	Biotechnology
Botany	Cell biology
Ecology	Entomology
Genetics	Histology
Immunology	Microbiology
Molecular biology	Neuroscience
Physiology	Zoology

Chemistry:

Biochemistry	Chemistry
Physical chemistry	Thermodynamics

Physics:

Astronomy	Physics

Math:

Applied mathematics	Biostatistics
Mathematics	Statistics

How the GPA is listed in the application

The grid has a row for "high school" if you received any college credit and rows for each year of college. After that, it has rows for Postbaccalaureate Undergraduate, Cumulative Undergraduate, and Graduate grades. Postbacccalaureate undergraduate grades will appear on a separate line in the grade grid, but these grades are used to calculate your overall average undergraduate GPAs. In addition to the "grade grid" (see figure below), each course you have taken is also listed in the section before the grade grid, with the corresponding grade you received. Any grade that is listed on your transcript must be listed on your application and factored into your GPA calculations. You do not compute your GPAs; the AMCAS® system does this for you to avoid any error. Students are required to list any courses they have taken as undergraduates or graduates and must list the grade received as it appears on the transcript. You must also list the credit hours earned as it appears on the transcript (hours, units, etc.), and AMCAS® will convert these grades to semester hours. Do not convert your grades and credit hours on your application. Students must submit transcripts from each school they attended even if they did not receive a degree. AMCAS® will compare your transcripts with the courses and grades you have listed, and everything must "match" perfectly or the processing of your application may be delayed.

AMCAS® grade grid example

	BCPM GPA	BCPM Hours	AO GPA	AO Hours	Total GPA	Total Hours
High School						
Freshman						
Sophomore						
Junior						
Senior						
Postbac Undergraduate						
Cumulative Undergraduate						
Graduate						
Supplemental Hours	P/F – Pass	P/F – Fail	A/P:	CLEP:	OTHER:	

Calculating your GPA yourself

Even though AMCAS® calculates your GPAs for you, it is still possible (and advisable) to have a rough idea of what these calculations will be. Also realize that AMCAS® calculates GPAs using semester hours so if you are on a quarter system, or any other credit system, you will need to convert your grades to semester hours to calculate your AMCAS® GPA. If you are not sure how to do this, you should contact your registrar or refer to the AMCAS® Grade Conversion Guide that is published annually.

Regardless of the grading system used, all grades will need to be converted to a traditional numeric grading scale that corresponds to standard letter grades as follows:

A   4.0
A-   3.7
B+   3.3
B   3.0
B-   2.7
C+   2.3
C   2.0
D+   1.7
D   1.0
D-   0.0
F   0.0

If your school has another grading system, such as Halfstep Grades, another four passing letter grade system, or percentage system, for example, you will again need to contact your registrar or refer to the AMCAS® Grade Conversion Chart for information on how these are converted.

What should be my GPA goal? What if my freshman year grades were awful?

Obviously, the higher your GPA, the better. However, the general ball park cut-off that medical schools use is an overall GPA of 3.5. That said, schools also pay attention to grade trends. Many students do poorly early in college simply because they are not prepared for the academic course load and don't have the maturity and time management and study skills to do well. As long as your grades trend upward, medical schools are sometimes willing to forgive a poor performance early in your early academic career. But, for the really competitive schools, academic excellence throughout college is essential.

If your undergraduate GPA is not competitive enough to gain admission to an allopathic medical school, you must decide if you will consider less competitive options such as osteopathic or off-shore medical schools, or if you want to attend a postbaccalaureate or special master's program to enhance your academics. These options are discussed elsewhere in the book.

What about withdrawals or pass/fail classes?

Every admissions officer knows that taking a class pass/ fail is the easy option. I therefore discourage applicants from taking classes pass/fail and advise never to take a prerequisite or science class pass/fail. Withdrawals are also not looked upon favorably. More than one to two withdrawals on a transcript can raise concern. So, try to drop classes (if you must) before "drop deadlines."

CHAPTER 3

THE MCAT®

Medical school admissions committees use the multiple choice, standardized MCAT® to determine if you have the scientific knowledge and intellectual skills to study medicine and succeed in medical school. A new MCAT® is being introduced in the spring of 2015. The MCAT2015® is different from its predecessor in many ways – length and number of questions, content, and the way it is scored. The MedEdits team participated in a webinar on the new test, and below we note and comment on some of the new, key features and offer our thoughts.

When should I take the MCAT®?

1. In making this decision, you first need to decide when you plan to start medical school.

Up to 40% of medical schools will accept only MCAT® scores that are no more than two years old. Only a handful of medical schools will consider MCAT® scores that are four years old, so you don't want to be in a situation where most medical schools consider your score "too old." Refer to the latest edition of Medical School

Admission Requirements published online by the AAMC for the most up to date information.

2. You then need to figure out when you will be ready to take the test. Never take the MCAT® without having all the prerequisites you need and adequate time to prepare well. Never rush your work to make an MCAT® date. It is best to be as well prepared as possible and to take the MCAT® as few times as possible. Ideally, an applicant should take the MCAT® once and do as well as he or she can.

MCAT2014®

The MCAT2014® had three sections: Biological Sciences (BS), Physical Sciences (PS), Verbal Reasoning (VR) and Trial Section (TS). Of these sections, your performance on BS and PS were the most important with VR following close behind. The writing sample that had originally been on the MCAT® was no longer included because few medical school admissions considered the results of this section for admission.

MCAT2015®

The MCAT® has been changed for several reasons. First, revisions have been made to reflect changes in medical education, new knowledge about the natural sciences and the skills now required of medical students and doctors to care for an increasingly diverse patient population. Admissions officers also want to ensure that prospective medical students have the analytical, scientific inquiry, and reasoning skills necessary to practice medicine; the new exam does a better job testing for this than the old MCAT®. Compared with its predecessors, the

MCAT2015® is a more multidisciplinary exam that tests knowledge and intellectual skills and the ability to integrate those skills. The shift is from testing what you know to evaluating how well you can apply what you have learned. The emphasis is on determining whether you can think like a scientist, with a new content area on Critical Analysis and Reasoning Skills Also added is a section on Psychological, Social and Biological Foundations of Behavior in recognition of the important roles of behavioral and sociocultural factors in health and illness.

The MCAT2015® has four sections: Biological & Biochemical Foundations of Living Systems, Chemical & Physical Foundations of Biological Systems, Psychological, Social & Biological Foundations of Behavior, and Critical Analysis and Reasoning Skills. Only the first three sections require specific prerequisites. The scientifically-based sections reflect the need for Scientific Foundations for Future Physicians (SFFP) competencies by having more interdisciplinary passages and requiring examinees to merge knowledge and apply problem-solving, scientific inquiry, and reasoning skills.

1. Biological & Biochemical Foundations of Living Systems (Bio/Biochem)*

This section tests knowledge of biologic and biochemical concepts as well as the ability to apply analytical, scientific inquiry, reasoning, and statistics skills to solve problems.

2. Chemical & Physical Foundations of Biological Systems: (Chem/Phys)*

This section tests knowledge of chemical and physical sciences and, as in section 1, the ability to apply analytical, scientific inquiry, reasoning ,and statistics to solve problems.

Sections 1 & 2 are collectively referred to as the natural sciences. Prerequisites for these sections are: Introductory biology, biochemistry (one semester only), inorganic (general) chemistry, organic chemistry & physics. About 75% of the content in sections 1 & 2 is the same as in the MCAT2014®.

3. Psychological, Social & Biological Foundations of Behavior: (Psych/Soc)* (prerequisites: Sociology, Psychology & Biology)

This completely new section of the MCAT2015® tests knowledge of psychology and sociology along with some basic biologic principles. This section was added to recognize the importance of social and behavioral determinants of health in the practice of medicine. Like the other sections, it tests the ability to apply analytical, scientific inquiry, reasoning ,and statistics to solve problems.

4. Critical Analysis and Reasoning Skills: (CARS*)

This section does not test a specific knowledge base or subjects. Instead, it evaluates the critical analysis and scientific reasoning skills required of medical students and physicians. This section covers topics such as ethics, population health, philosophy, and cross-cultural studies.

More information about the MCAT2015® can be found here: www.aamc.org/mcat2015. I also encourage applicants to read all material about the MCAT2015® that the AAMC publishes. I consider this the best source for information about the exam because this is where all updates about the MCAT2015®, including topics covered, will be posted as the exam is refined. Full length practice tests and preparation materials will also be available.

*MCAT2015® section abbreviations were made up by the author since the AAMC had not yet determined section abbreviations when this book was written

How is the MCAT® scored?

MCAT2015® scoring has been completely changed in a conscious shift away from the old model and toward a new way of thinking that recognizes that those at the center of the score range—instead of just the "top of the curve"–typically have done well in medical school and finish in four to five years. This reflects the emphasis the AAMC is putting on the holistic admissions process and choosing students who can best serve the patients who need serving, not necessarily the students who have the highest GPAs and scores.

Your MCAT® score will consist of five scores – one for each section and a "total" composite score. Each section will be scored from 118-132 with 125 the midpoint or "top" of the curve. Overall exam score will be reported from 472 to 528 with 500 as midpoint or "top" of the curve.

On questioning, the MCAT® team revealed that the 50th percentile on the current version of the test reflects a score of 25-26, and the new 500 score also is the 50th percentile. Currently, few students with a score of 25-26 are admitted to allopathic medical schools. However, 90% of students with 25-26 MCAT® scores who were admitted took five years to graduate rather than four. The MCAT® team, when pressed, said that by focusing at the middle of the curve schools will capture students who can "do well" in medical school and graduate in four to five years.

Percentile rank and confidence bands will be included with the score report to help admissions committees further interpret the scores.

The score report for the 2015 exam will be much more detailed than in the past in an effort to highlight an applicant's strengths and weaknesses more clearly. It will include "confidence bands," which indicate a range of an applicant's possible scores on any given day. For example, if you earn a score of 125 in one section, the confidence band would be 124 – 126. The AAMC hopes that confidence bands will help admissions committees see the range of scores an applicant might achieve on a good, bad, or average day.

The report will also indicate how the applicant's percentile scores compares with those of other test takers.

A visual "score profile" will provide someone who is reviewing the score profile a visual idea of the applicant's strengths and weaknesses. The AAMC has made available a sample score report to educate applicants about score reporting and show them how these score reports will look to admissions committees.

Given that MCAT® performance historically predicts USMLE scores and that USMLE scores are an important consideration for residency program directors during the selection process, I do think admissions committees will make an effort to conform to this new scale and way of thinking. My sense is that they will consider the "top (or midpoint) of the curve" for what it numerically represents – the 50th percentile– and try to recruit and matriculate students who score better than 500, especially in the new sections. Both UGPAs and MCAT® scores are strong predictors of academic performance in medical school so this new scoring system will require adaptation but may not truly change the way admissions committees conduct their processes.

Each major section of the MCAT2014® was graded on a 15 point scale. The highest score you could receive in each section was a 15 and the lowest a 1. The composite range on the MCAT2014® was 3-45 and the maximum total score a student could earn was a 45. When looked at more carefully, the MCAT2015® scale is also a 1-15 scale, but the entire scale has been shifted with higher numbers (118-132)! The composite range of scores one could earn will be 472-528. Extrapolate these numbers and the "new 30" the MCAT2015® is 508 (127 x 4). The maximum score a student can earn on the MCAT2015® is 528.

Let's explain this further:

MCAT2015® approximations:

1. Four sections
2. Score of 118-132 in each section
3. The "new 10" in each section is 127
4. Composite score that can be earned: 427-528
5. Therefore, the "new 30" is 127 x 4 or 508

Your score is based on the number of questions you answer correctly. This number of correct answers in each multiple choice section. Each correct answer has the same value, and incorrectly answered questions do not count against you (so it is fine to guess!).

What is considered a good score?

Quite obviously, the higher you score on the MCAT® the better, but a composite score of 30 on the MCAT2014® is generally considered the score needed to gain admission to medical school. However, retrospective studies have shown that a composite score of 27 on the MCAT2014® predicts that an applicant will successfully graduate from medical school.

The AAMC will publish a conversion table for medical school admissions officers to "convert' 2014 scores to 2015 scores and vice versa once more data are available. Based on the data that was available when this book was written, it is not clear what "the new 30" will be on the MCAT2015®; however, as already mentioned, we anticipate that "the new 30" will be a composite score of about 508. Applicants should follow the MedEdits blog where we will keep applicants up to date with developments as this information is released.

The distribution of the three section scores was also important in evaluating MCAT2014® performance, with more "even" distribution considered better. It was also preferable if a candidate's lowest score was in verbal reasoning (especially for any score below a 10) rather than in one of the two science sections. We do not yet know how medical school admissions committees will interpret the MCAT2015® scores, but I think it is safe to assume that, once again, they will give more weight to the two natural science sections.

Consider these applicants' scores, all of whom earned a composite score of 30:

Applicant A: VR: 8 BS: 11 PS: 11
Applicant B: VR: 11 BS: 8 PS: 11
Applicant C: VR: 10 BS: 10 PS: 10

In this scenario, applicant A is in good shape. He scored 11 in both science sections, which predicts he will do well in medical school. In contrast, Applicant B might concern some admissions committees. Even though

Applicant B's composite score is the same as Applicant A's, Applicant B earned an 8 in the biological sciences, in which proficiency is essential to do well as a medical student. Ah, Applicant C. Applicant C earned 10s across the board, which impresses admissions committees – this applicant has no deficiencies.

As a general rule, it is best not to score below an 8 (about a 125 on the MCAT2015®) in any section since some medical schools do not interview applicants with scores in this range. But many schools review each applicant individually. The MCAT® is only one piece of the puzzle and is considered together with the student's academic performance, accomplishments, written documents, and letters of reference. I have had many clients with MCAT2014® scores of 27 who have been accepted to US allopathic medical schools, and some have even earned "7s" or "8s" in the science sections.

At the time this book was written, the MCAT2015® was not yet being administered. Please visit the MedEdits blog and Facebook page where we will post scenarios similar to the one above for the MCAT2015®.

If you want to know where you stand relative to national data, refer to the AAMC MCAT®/GPA grid to see what percentage of applicants in your range are accepted to medical school.

When is the MCAT® given?

The MCAT® is offered every month of the year except February and December. Exact dates vary from year to year and new test dates are frequently added so be sure to check testing dates carefully by referring to the AAMC

MCAT® scheduling page: (web: https://www.aamc.org/ students/applying/mcat/reserving/). You receive your scores 30 to 35 days after you take the MCAT®, but for the first few times the test is given, it will take up to two months for scores to be released.

When should I take the MCAT2015®?

As mentioned at the beginning of this chapter, it is ideal to take the test only after you have completed all of the prerequisites and have adequately prepared for the exam. Again, I suggest that applicants take the test only once, if possible. Most medical schools will not accept scores older than two to three years

On test day you should feel you have mastered the material and skills needed to perform your best and be 100% confident that you can do so. To accomplish this, try to be in an ideal frame of mind on test day. For example, rushing to finish final exams and then taking the MCAT® two days after graduating from college might not be the best idea. You want to be well rested and as confident as possible on test day.

If you plan to take the MCAT® during the application year, the latest test date I recommend is June, but a winter or early spring exam is preferable because it allows the applicant's medical school application to be reviewed earlier in the admissions cycle. An earlier test date also helps students choose a school list since school selection is largely dependent on MCAT® performance; an earlier test date also gives an applicant more time to devise a "retake" strategy if this becomes necessary.

However, some students can take the MCAT® in July or August of the application year and get accepted, but typically these students have exceptional scores (above 35) so a later review of their application won't be detrimental. For most applicants, a mid – to late-summer MCAT® date can hurt their chances of acceptance since most medical schools have rolling admissions and won't review an application until they have received the applicant's MCAT® scores.

How should I prepare?

When students ask me how to prepare, I first ask them, "How did you prepare for the SAT® and what worked?" At this point, most students know their weaknesses and have an idea of how they learn best (see "A few MCAT® pointers"). I suggest that students take at least three months to study for the MCAT®. The material that is tested is typically covered in undergraduate courses. How best to prepare will vary from applicant to applicant and there is no one right way. Here are some possibilities:

1. Review on your own. If you are a good self-studier and have excellent time management and organizational skills, buying or borrowing review books and studying on your own could be a good option. Many excellent review books are available if you need to supplement what you have learned in your prerequisite courses. Many students have the discipline to self-study and incorporate the AAMC practice tests in their study plan (see below).

2. Commercial prep course. Most often, students prepare for the exam by enrolling in MCAT® review courses, which are either live or online. These courses do not vary tremendously in quality and their effectiveness depends on the each individual

teacher's talent, which is often difficult to assess before a course. But whatever the effectiveness of the course, taking it forces a student to stay on schedule and create a study plan, which in itself has value. In my experience, these courses sometimes offer initial "diagnostic tests," which tend to "underscore" applicants and then offer "simulated tests," which "overscore" applicants. I am not sure why testing companies use this strategy, but perhaps they are trying to make applicants nervous initially to motivate them to study and then to boost students' confidence before test day. Regardless, evaluate your performance on commercial practice tests with a grain of salt and place a higher value on your AAMC practice test performance (see below).

3. Private tutoring. When I took the MCAT®, no one hired private tutors, but this is becoming more common. It might be beneficial to seek out a talented tutor for "problem spots" if you need some intensive study for certain areas. For some applicants, private tutoring for every section might be a possible and expensive option.

4. Study plan. Regardless of how you prepare, it is essential to have an organized study plan to ensure you get through all of the material before the exam. As mentioned, I recommend that students take at least three months to study for the MCAT®. Being well prepared for the MCAT® is essential, and required preparation time will vary from student to student. Be honest with yourself and devote the time you need to do well on the exam even if this means postponing your planned application year.

5. Practice tests. The AAMC offers practice tests for applicants, which are real, "retired" MCAT2014® exams. I recommend that applicants take all of these tests by incorporating them into their study schedules. Performance on these tests is the most accurate predictor of how a student will perform on test day. Go to the following link to order practice tests: (web: https://www.aamc. org/students/applying/mcat/preparing/85158/ orderingpracticetests_mcat.html). The AAMC will also offer full length practice MCAT2015® tests. The first full length practice MCAT2015 exam will be available in 2015.

6. AAMC resources. The AAMC provides many resources for applicants as they prepare for the MCAT®, including a portal of resources offered by undergraduate university professors. In addition, in collaboration with Khan Academy and the Robert Wood Johnson Foundation, AAMC will offer free lectures and tutorials to help students prepare. Consult the AAMC MCAT® web pages to stay up to date with what is available.

A few MCAT® pointers

Remember: Each section contains experimental questions that do not count towards your score. (At the time this book was written, however, it was not confirmed that the MCAT2015® would have experimental questions.)

Don't be afraid to guess. You are evaluated only on those answers answered correctly.

Remember: You can change answers within each

section, but once you are finished with a section you can not return to that section.

Before your exam, read MCAT Essentials®, which the AAMC publishes annually.

Register for your exam early. Testing centers have limited capacities and fill up early!

How can I register?

All MCAT® registrations are done online at https://services.aamc.org/20/mcat/. The fee to register in 2015 is $300. This is a $25 increase over the 2014 price to account for the longer test day.

Fee Assistance Program recipients will have a reduced cost of $115.

Be sure to read the AAMC publication, MCAT Essentials®, which is free and revised annually, before you register for the exam to stay up to date about registration policies and fees.

Can I register for two tests at a time?

You can register for only one MCAT® at a time and you are allowed to take the MCAT® up to three times in each calendar year, something I don't advise even though in theory, you can take the MCAT® an unlimited number of times. You can register for another MCAT® exam 48 hours after your scheduled time and date. However, students rarely improve by quickly "signing up for another test date" unless they can easily identify a reason why they may have underperformed (see "Should I retake the MCAT®?" below).

What happens on test day?

The MCAT®, a computerized test, is offered at specific testing centers. Review each testing center's rules and regulations before taking the exam and make a practice trip to the testing center before your actual exam day. Be sure you travel during the same time and day of the week so you don't underestimate how long the trip will take. Nothing causes more anxiety than being late for an exam. Be sure you have the correct identification needed to take your test and allow time for test center check in, including security issues.

MCAT2015® approximate testing time breakdown

- Examinee Agreement 8 minutes
- Tutorial (optional) 10 minutes
- Chemical and Physical Foundations of Biological Systems: 59 items, 95 minutes
- Break (optional) 10 minutes
- Critical Analysis and Reasoning Skills: 53 items, 90 minutes
- Mid-Exam Break (optional) 30 minutes
- Biological and Biochemical Foundations of Living Systems: 59 items, 95 minutes
- Break (optional) 10 minutes
- Psychological, Social, and Biological Foundations of Behavior: 59 items, 95 minutes
- Void Question 5 minutes
- Satisfaction Survey (optional) 5 minutes
- Total Content Time 6 hours, 15 minutes
- Total "Seated" Time* Approx. 7 hours, 33 minutes

Should I retake the MCAT®?

This question is tough to answer, especially because the answer varies with the applicant. If you have a good score (above an MCAT2014® 30 with no section score below an 8 or an MCAT2015® score of 508 with no section score below about 125), and you gave studying your full attention for at least three months, retaking the test is unlikely to improve your score. The only caveat to this general principle is if you can clearly identify something you did wrong; if so, and you feel that retaking the test will improve your score by at least two to three points on MCAT2014® or four points on MCAT2015®, then consider a retake.

- If one of the following scenarios applies to you, consider retaking the MCAT®:

- You were really sick when you took the exam.

- You didn't prepare adequately for either the entire exam or one section on which you scored an 8 or below (about 125 on MCAT2015).

- You were flustered because of an upsetting experience the morning of the exam, such as an accident on your way to the testing center, a bad flight, or a fight with a loved one.

Be sure to consider the timing of a retake, however. If you are in your "application year," remember that a summer or fall exam date will delay review of your application and unless your score bumps up significantly, the retake will cause your application to be reviewed later, which might have a negative effect on your application.

For how long are my scores valid?

As mentioned, medical schools generally require that your MCAT® scores be no more than two to three years old. You should check requirements for each individual medical school. However, every MCAT® result, regardless of how old, will be listed on your application, something that comes as a surprise to some applicants who mistakenly believe that when scores "expire," they are no longer seen.

If I take the MCAT® more than once, will medical schools consider my highest score?

Each medical school reviews MCAT® scores in its own way. Some medical schools say they average all scores, some say they take the highest score earned from each section across multiple tests, while others say they consider the highest composite exam score. Regardless of the formula medical schools use, the results of MCATs® taken since 2003 are automatically released to them and are subject to their scrutiny, which means, for example, that medical schools will see even that 22 you got three years ago.

The larger the gap between two scores, the more likely a first lower test score will be considered "not representative of your abilities." For example, using MCAT2014® scores, if you earned a 23 on your first test and a 37 on the second, the reviewer is likely to assume that, "something happened" on the day you earned the 23 since these scores were so vastly different. But, the difference between a 29 and a 31 is more subtle. Every student has a certain "range" within which he or she will score on any given day so a 29 and a 31 may both be viewed as fair representations of a student's true abilities. The

MCAT2015® score reports are intended to provide a more accurate depiction of an applicant's abilities by visually depicting these ranges.

A few final suggestions and reminders

1. Never take the MCAT® as a "practice run" or without being fully prepared. Be sure you have taken all of your prerequisites and have studied adequately before taking the exam.

2. Many students have difficulty with verbal reasoning. Be sure to get through this section of the test. Many students get low scores on verbal reasoning simply because they don't complete the entire section.

3. Avoid taking the MCAT® multiple times. If you take the MCAT® more than twice, and at least two of your scores are in the same range, the higher score is less "convincing." For example, if your MCAT2014® score is a 29, a 30, and then a 34, admissions committees are more likely to view the 34 as an outlier.

Taking the MCAT® with accommodations

Students may apply for testing accommodations through the AAMC and, if you have a disability or medical condition that requires you to have more time to do well, I encourage you to apply for accommodations. Even though your score will have a small asterisk next to it on your AMCAS application, many reviewers rarely notice this or ask about it on interviews, especially if you score well. Students who require accommodations will take the MCAT2015® over two to three days. To see what documentation is needed to receive accommodations, visit the MCAT® with Accommodations portion of the AAMC website (web: https://www.aamc.org/students/applying/mcat/46436/accommodations/). I have worked with many students who received testing accommodations and were accepted to medical school. It is important to know that you must be evaluated for a learning disability or ADD/ADHD within three years of your desired test. Psychiatric disabilities must be evaluated six months before taking the exam, but exceptions are made depending on the diagnosis. Medical conditions must be evaluated six months before the test date without exception. It is best to apply for accommodations early since this process can take time.

CHAPTER 4

FUTURE ADMISSIONS CONSIDERATIONS

When the MCAT2015® was in development, many people advocated testing applicants for personal competencies. While this wasn't instituted, the use of Situational Judgement Tests (SJTs) is being explored. SJTs are scenario based and test applicants on how they react to, and behave in, certain situations. Scenarios might be presented in written, animated or live video formats.

Future AMCAS applications may also ask applicants to reflect on specific competencies For example, with regard to cultural competence, applicants would be asked to write an entry about a specific instance during which they demonstrated this competency.

While this is purely speculative on my part, I also think admissions committees might consider doing digital footprint checks on applicants. With so many people using online social forums (via their real names and aliases), and because so much useful information – some of which might determine an admissions decision – can be found relatively easily online, I believe that routine digital footprints will ultimately become part of routine job and admissions screenings.

CHAPTER 5

ACTIVITIES AND EXTRACURRICULARS

In what activities should I participate?

Medical schools like to see that students have diverse involvements in areas of research, clinical exposure, teaching, community service, and employment. Most students find it difficult to have experience in each of these areas, however, so don't feel you must participate in all of the listed activities in this book. Medical schools would rather see deep and significant involvement that takes place over time rather than superficial involvement in multiple activities. For example, single day experiences carry less weight than activities that show genuine commitment and learning. In fact, I discourage applicants from listing single-day experiences on the application itself since medical schools often view these as "filler experiences" that only an applicant without more meaningful involvements would list. Admission committee members also like to see that your involvements make logical sense and reflect your interests and the evolution of these interests. I must also point out that students should not take on more activities than they can handle; don't do anything that might jeopardize your academic performance, which is always the most important ingredient for gaining admission to medical school.

How should you seek out experiences? While formal "programs" often are available for a variety of activities, I encourage students to seek out specific places or organizations where they would like to find an opportunity. For example, if you are an athlete interested in orthopedics, call the orthopedics department of a nearby academic institution and ask if any research opportunities are available. Or, if you want to volunteer at a nursing home close to your home, call the nursing home and inquire about opportunities.

Activities medical schools most like to see

Clinical exposure

All medical schools want to see that you have varied clinical exposure. This can take the form of doctor shadowing, volunteering in a free clinic, or working abroad in some capacity. Some applicants have difficulty getting accepted to medical school because they may have extensive basic science research but have never shadowed a physician. It is a tough sell to say you want to be a doctor if you have never set foot in a doctor's office or a hospital. Obviously, as a student, you won't be given any clinical responsibilities, but admissions committees want to be sure that you understand what it means to practice medicine in a variety of settings.

I often suggest that students seek out shadowing experiences in emergency departments (EDs). I am not suggesting this because I am an emergency physician but because emergency departments are open 24/7, are always busy, and have a variety of patients with varied clinical presentations. You will also have the chance to formally observe many different specialists since the ED is often the hub of any hospital and consultants from other specialties visit the ED to care for patients.

Another great clinical alternative is to become an emergency medical technician. This is one of the few domestic experiences that allows students to have contact with patients. Becoming an emergency department scribe, where you act as the physician's assistant by taking notes, also presents a comprehensive clinical experience that allows you to acquire medical knowledge and an intimate understanding of how medicine is practiced, the doctor-patient relationship, and how hospitals operate.

If you prefer a different clinical setting where you can really have some hands-on and valuable experiences, consider volunteering in a hospice or nursing home. Places such as this often are filled with patients in need of company, and I find that students have very meaningful experiences in these settings.

If you plan on applying to osteopathic medical schools, you must shadow an osteopathic physician.

Research

Most medical schools, even those that are not major academic medical centers, want applicants to have research experience. The type of research doesn't really matter, but most students engage in some type of basic science research (either for credit, during a summer, or for employment) or clinical research. However, research in other disciplines will also allow you to learn how to think critically, analyze data, evaluate the literature, solve problems, and ask and then answer a question through experimentation. If you can't find a basic science or clinical research experience, consider research in another discipline of interest – psychology, art history, anthropology – or whatever else piques your curiosity. What you learn through research in any discipline can be applied to future research endeavors and help you to practice evidence – based medicine and to evaluate current studies, which will be necessary throughout your medical education, training, and career. Medical schools are placing more and more value on the importance of scientific inquiry, analytical skills, and the ability to apply knowledge practically as evidenced by the MCAT2015® changes. Therefore, significant research experience will be more, and not less, important in coming years.

Teaching

A career in medicine will always involve teaching even if you don't plan to become a medical school professor. Why? As a physician, you will always educate your patients and their loved ones so acquiring the skills to communicate difficult concepts to others who have less knowledge than you do is important. Many students serve as teaching assistants for courses in which they performed well, or tutor children in their local community in either academic disciplines, athletics, or the arts. Teaching people who have backgrounds different than your own is also valuable. As our country becomes more diverse, knowing how to communicate across cultures is becoming increasingly important. Showing that you have nurtured these skills as a premedical student can be an asset.

Community service/volunteer work

Lending your services to help others in need is always a worthwhile endeavor. Medical schools are seeking people who are compassionate, caring, and empathetic so demonstrating these traits through community service or volunteer work is important. Medical schools also seek applicants who want to help others in need, including the underserved. Physicians also play significant roles in their communities, so medical schools value students who have a demonstrated a commitment to serve their community.

Service work can be performed in medical and non-medical settings, and both are considered desirable. As mentioned above, medical schools value volunteering in a free clinic, nursing home, hospital, or hospice. Spending time in non-clinical settings, such as a soup kitchen, a tutoring program, or helping to build homes for those who are less fortunate, also demonstrates a commitment to serve.

As with teaching, community service work often presents golden opportunities to work with different populations and cultures. This allows you to showcase cultural competency and develop communication skills that are increasingly important to medical school admissions committees.

Work experience

Nothing takes the place of understanding the value of a dollar and what it means to earn money. Medical schools respect students who have work experiences. If you worked as a store clerk or a waitperson, for example, you understand the importance of customer service, how to work with different people of different backgrounds and cultures, and how to manage conflict in a nonacademic setting. Work experiences might also make you more appreciative of your education and opportunities. As a physician, you will also work with diverse individuals in collaborative settings so having real world work experience in any arena is significant.

I find that people who must work to help support themselves often shy away from writing about such topics in their applications when, in reality, this commitment may distinguish them from other applicants. Having a part time job while going to school is not easy, and medical school admissions committees want to know about such extenuating circumstances. Students who work to help support themselves are often very appreciative of what they have and are more mature, better able to manage their time, and very hard working.

Experience with people from different backgrounds

As a physician, you will work with people from different cultures and socioeconomic backgrounds. Admissions committees want to know that you have an open mind and can appreciate and recognize differences in people. In other words, they want to know that you are "culturally competent," meaning you have the sensitivity, skills, and aptitude to work with and care for people who have beliefs, traditions, perspectives, and ideals that are different from your own. Most relevant activities, with the exception perhaps of traditional bench research, can take place in a variety of settings that will allow you to demonstrate these ideals. Stepping outside your comfort zone and working with people and in settings that are not familiar also demonstrates your adaptability and inclination to work with and help people from a variety of backgrounds.

Other

Medical school admissions committees also want to know that you have varied interests. Do you excel in the performing arts, or athletics, or do you have an unusual (or not so unusual) hobby? The more dimension you can add to your candidacy, the better. Medical schools hope to attract students who can excel not only in a rigorous scientifically based curriculum but who are well rounded and have interests outside of the classroom and the lab.

Themes

Medical school admissions committees value seeing themes in a student's background only when a theme does not seem forced or contrived. For example, let's say you have an academic interest in Hispanic studies. A medical school admissions committee would appreciate seeing that not only did you pursue your intellectual interests but that you also volunteered in a clinic located in a Hispanic community and did research in public health. It is great when an applicant can demonstrate a logical flow between experiences and can explain how one interest led to another. If you have a strong interest in soccer, for example, maybe you established an inner city program teaching children to play.

Key qualities and characteristics for admission

As you select the experiences in which you will be involved, keep in mind the key qualities and characteristics that medical school admissions committees are seeking in applicants (see "Personal competencies, qualities, and characteristics medical schools value"). Keep this as a checklist to make sure you "hit" most of these items by choosing experiences that will allow you to demonstrate these qualities and characteristics.

Personal competencies, qualities, and characteristics medical schools value

For every step of the medical school admissions process, you will be evaluated for the following qualities and characteristics. I will refer back to this list several times.

Able to cope with adversity
Able to improve
Able to lead
Able to reason
Able to think critically and analytically
Able to overcome obstacles
Able to work as an effective team member
Adaptable
Altruistic
Aware of others
Committed to medicine
Skilled in communicating – orally , in writing, and by being a good listener
Compassionate
Culturally competent
Dependable
Eager to help others
Disciplined
Empathetic
Ethical
Skilled at interacting with others
Honest
Acts with integrity
Intellectually able
Intellectually curious
Mature
Motivated to pursue a career in medicine
Persistent

Professional
Resilient
Respectful of others
Relishes scientific inquiry
Sensitive to others
Socially aware
Has a strong work ethic
Has upstanding values and ideals
Warm

CHAPTER 6

LETTERS OF REFERENCE

Obtaining strong letters of reference from a variety of individuals is key to getting accepted to medical school. Admissions committees want to know that other people believe in you and your abilities and that you have the qualities and characteristics listed elsewhere in this book to be a great medical student and physician. Ideally, your letters of reference will enthusiastically support your candidacy. It isn't always easy to know who writes "good" letters, however, and writing an excellent letter of reference is indeed an art; some people are fundamentally better letter writers than others. You may know of professors who have reputations for writing especially good letters while others may be known for writing mediocre letters. Most often, unfortunately, students do not know which are which.

How can I prepare to get good letters of reference?

I encourage applicants to think of every professor and supervisor as a potential letter writer. This means that throughout college or your post-graduate work you will go to office hours, pay attention in class, and do your best to stand out. If you have a professor during your sophomore year whom you think will support your candidacy but you don't plan to apply to medical school for two years, you should ask this professor, after the class ends, if he would be willing to write a strong letter of reference for you when you apply to medical school. The professor may offer to write the letter at the end of the class, in which case your prehealth office will hold the letter until you are ready to apply, or you can submit the letter to a "letter service" (see below) until it is time to submit your letters. Alternatively, the letter writer may offer to write the letter during the year you plan to apply to medical school. In this case, be sure to stay in touch with the professor until he writes this letter. Keep him up to date with your accomplishments so he won't forget you and will then be able to write a letter of reference with more depth.

What about committee letters?

Most undergraduate institutions have premedical "committee letters" and if this includes your school, you must have one of these letters in your medical school application. Medical schools see a "red flag" when an applicant from a school known to have committee letters is missing this piece of documentation.

Be aware that some undergraduate premedical committees won't automatically write premedical committee letters for every student who wants to go to medical school; the committee members will decide if they support your decision to apply. They often base these decisions on GPA cut-offs or other criteria that predict your success in being admitted to medical school. Undergraduate colleges are concerned with their "student success statistics," and it therefore may behoove them to support only those candidates who are likely to be successful in the medical school admissions process.

Committee letters come in two forms: Most summarize your background and candidacy and, more important, "rank" you at the end of the letter relative to other premedical students from the school. This is usually done in code; for example, the top quarter of applicants are "outstanding," the next quarter are "excellent," the third quarter are "good," and the last quarter are "acceptable." This "ranking sentence" is often the most important part of the committee letter, assuming that the rest of your application gives a comprehensive overview of your candidacy. Other committee letters may summarize your letters of reference, but they all include a "ranking sentence."

What if I graduated from college years ago and the committee doesn't know me?

Exceptions can be made for students who attended a college that had a premedical committee letter but the student was not premed while at the school. In these situations, no medical school would expect you to have a committee letter.

Who should write individual letters of reference?

As a general rule, I suggest that students obtain at least two letters of reference from science professors. This advice concerns some students because they are often part of large classes and know the teaching assistants (TAs) better than the professors. But because admissions committees do not value the opinion of TAs alone, I suggest that in this situation you ask the TA if he would write the letter and find out if the professor would be willing to cosign it. I also recommend that students have at least one letter from a non-science professor, if possible. Other letters, especially those that come from letter writers who worked with you in medically and scientifically related pursuits, will also support your candidacy. Students can also ask for letters from the following:

Research supervisor/mentor
Humanities professor
Extracurricular supervisor
Physician with whom they worked or shadowed
Volunteer supervisor
Work supervisor

I recommend that students who are applying to osteopathic medical schools also obtain a letter of reference from an osteopathic physician even though most osteopathic medical schools do not consider this a requirement.

Should I get a letter from a "big name"?

Letters from "big names" usually are not useful unless the student has worked with the "big name" directly. It is best to obtain letters from people who know you well and can write about you in a detailed and knowledgeable manner. Superficial or mediocre letters, even from "big names," can hurt your candidacy since they imply that you have no one else to ask.

How many letters should I get?

I suggest obtaining a minimum of four letters or reference and a maximum of eight. The more quality endorsements of your candidacy that you have, the stronger your application will be. Having many people from different sources saying great things about you gives you more credibility. Do not get numerous letters from individuals who do not know you well. For example, four outstanding letters is a better option than four outstanding letters with three mediocre letters that will dilute your overall candidacy endorsement. I advise students to have a minimum of two "science letters" (from professors or research mentors), one humanities letter, and one letter from someone in a supervisory position from an extracurricular activity or work experience. AMCAS allows students to upload up to 10 letters. Keep in mind that you also have the option to send specific letters to specific medical schools. For example, let's say you have a research advisor who said he will write you a great letter for your alma mater, tailored just for that school. You could upload that letter and designate the letter only for that specific medical school.

When should I ask for letters of reference?

You should ask for letters of reference in January or February of the application year unless you have already requested them at the end of a class as noted above. Since letters of reference often delay completion of your medical school application, it is best to give your letter writers plenty of time to compose a letter.

Do I ask for a personal meeting when I ask for a letter of reference?

This question has no "one size fits all" answer.

For example, when I was an associate director of residents and my residents asked me to write letters of reference, I did not feel the need to meet with them because I knew them so well after working with them directly for three years. I simply asked for an up-to-date curriculum vitae (CV or resume) so I could review accomplishments of which I might not have been aware. I did not know the medical students with whom I worked as well, however, because typically we worked together only briefly. So, when medical students requested a letter or reference, I generally asked to meet with them so I could ask some targeted questions that would allow me to write a stronger and more sincere letter of reference.

The lesson here is to individualize the manner in which you ask for letters of reference. If you don't know your letter writer well, call him or an assistant to schedule a meeting. At this meeting, which could be in person or over the phone, ask if he would be willing to write you a strong letter of reference. The key word here is strong; you have to hope that anyone who feels she cannot write you an excellent letter of reference will be honest and say so. Some people may not be forthcoming about not wanting to write a letter of reference, however. If you sense even a hint of reluctance from someone whom you ask to write a letter, move on and seek out someone else. Hesitation implies that she either doesn't support your candidacy, is too busy, or isn't comfortable writing letters of reference.

Assuming your letter writer is willing to support your candidacy, ask what materials he would like from you to make this task easier. Many individuals will need no prompting to convey this information, but if your letter writer doesn't ask, consider sending him an up-to-date CV via email before your meeting. Some premedical advisors suggest bringing a hard copy "portfolio" to your letter writer that includes your CV, personal statement, and any additional materials that might be helpful. Since most people in academics are now accustomed to communicating via email, many prefer to receive electronic versions of all documents rather than hard copies but, again, ask your letter writer about his preferences.

If your letter writer asks for a personal or a brief autobiographical statement, do not feel that you must provide what will be the final draft of your medical school personal statement; the letter writer simply wants a more comprehensive sense of who you are, which will allow her to write a substantial letter.

For letter writers whom you know well, it is acceptable to email them and ask if they would be willing to write you a strong letter of reference and ask how they would like to proceed; would they like to meet with you, speak with you, or see a CV or personal statement?

Always waive your right to see letters

AMCAS® asks you to waive your right to read your letters, and you should always agree to do so. Waiving your right protects letter writers in case they want to include something less than outstanding about you. Nonetheless, many letter writers, on their own, show you the letter they wrote on your behalf. This is their choice, and you are not breaking any rules if the letter writer initiates the contact. I often sent letters of reference I wrote to applicants; since applicants don't get positive feedback all that often, I wanted my students and residents to be aware of how highly I thought of them.

CHAPTER 7

APPLICATION TIMELINE

Applicants often wonder when during their undergraduate career they should apply to medical school. Be aware that the application process itself takes about 15 months so students apply in June the year before they plan to matriculate and actually matriculate the following August. For example, if you apply to medical school in June 2017, you won't actually matriculate until August 2018.

Here is a very general application timetable:

1. June: Submit medical school application
2. June – August: Complete medical school secondary applications
3. August – April: Medical school interviews
4. October 15 – August: Get accepted to medical school
5. August: Matriculate!

"Traditional" applicants are those who apply to medical school at the end of the junior year of college. As indicated in greater detail in this book, fewer and fewer applicants will be "traditional," especially with the increased number of prerequisites needed to take the MCAT2015. I find that most applicants apply at the end of the senior year of college and take one gap year during the application year itself.

CHAPTER 8

DECIDING TO TAKE A GAP YEAR (OR TWO!)

The average age of medical school matriculants was 24 (both men and women) in 2012, an all time high, which suggests that most successful applicants to medical school are "nontraditional." Based on our experience with MedEdits' clients, students who are "nontraditional" – taking one or more years away from formal academics after graduating college, tend to do better in the admissions process. Why? With so many prerequisites to take, MCAT® studying, and gaining the necessary extracurricular experiences, many students simply don't have the time to fit everything in to apply at the end of junior year as a "traditional" student. This is not to say that the traditional student cannot do well. However, many students prefer to have "less" stress by spacing out college studying, MCAT® studying, and gaining experiences.

With the larger number of prerequisites the MCAT2015® calls for, taking at least one "gap year" becomes almost a necessity for many applicants. So many applicants now apply at the end of the senior year of college, take a "gap year," and matriculate one year after graduating college. To engage in more meaningful work, some applicants take two "gap years." An added benefit to a gap year for many applicants, in addition to strengthening their candidacy, is to gain some experience in the "real world" and also become more mature in the process. These applicants often fare better in the application process although there is no data to back up this anecdotal observation. I find that some parents are uncomfortable with the idea of a gap year, concerned their child might get "off track." In reality however, realizing the need to take a gap year or two often shows good judgment and decision making and can strengthen an applicant's overall candidacy.

Should I apply in junior or senior year of college—or take a "gap year"?

Students should apply to medical school only when they are 100% ready, and many applicants need additional time to improve their candidacies with regard either to academics or to medically related pursuits depending on where your deficiencies or weaknesses might be. Others appreciate that the medical school application process is complex and time consuming and realize they would fare better by having more time. Whether to wait a year or more to apply is a personal decision, and applicants must be realistic and honest with themselves about their competitiveness and whether extra time would allow them to improve their candidacy and produce a great application. According to AAMC® surveys, about 50% of medical school matriculants are now taking at least one gap year between college and medical school. I speculate that with the increasing MCAT2015 prerequisites the average age of medical school matriculants will continue to rise.

What do students typically do during a gap year or two?

What do applicants do during a gap year? Many things, but keep in mind that a gap year is not the time to explore your non medical interests. Admissions committees want to see that you are doing something valuable related to science, medicine, or community service. The applicant with a low GPA, for example, might choose to pursue an advanced degree or a special master's program. An applicant with a weaker extracurricular profile might pursue a specific interest (public health, nutrition, global health) which could also provide the opportunity for academic enhancement for those who might need it. Another applicant might have little research or clinical exposure so might choose to strengthen his applicant in those arenas.

Here is a list of what some applicants do during a gap year:

1. Research – basic science or clinical
2. Teaching – in underserved areas. Some applicants do Teach for America and take more than one year off
3. Public health work – research, work in clinics
4. Formal education programs – master's in public health, nutrition, global health, or science
5. Clinical work – working as an EMT, scribe, or medical assistant

Applicants might also supplement the work they do with weekly clinical shadowing experiences or volunteer work. I do not recommend longer term work internationally during the application year itself since this can make travel for interviews complex and expensive.

What are the other benefits of at least one "gap" year?

Students who take a gap tend to be more mature, more confident, and have more to write about in their applications and talk about on interviews. Sometimes applicants who have had more experiences are simply more interesting people who have more poise, act more professional, and may seem better prepared for a career in medicine.

Future considerations

At this time, medical schools consider traditional, nontraditional, and former career applicants as a single cohort. I wonder if in the future admissions committees will consider each of these groups as a unique entity as I believe they should. Just as medical schools often consider underrepresented minorities and economically underprivileged candidates in distinct groups, the same should be true based on an applicant's life experience, I believe, since more mature applicants often have a distinct advantage when applying to and interviewing for medical school

Choosing a Special Master's Program

If you want to apply to medical school but don't think you have the GPA to be accepted to a US allopathic medical school, or if you applied to medical school and were not accepted, consider attending a special master's program. These programs are specifically designed for applicants who want to improve their candidacies for medical school. Most require an MCAT® and do have minimum MCAT® and GPA requirements. Some special master's programs are one year while others are two. Special master's students typically take classes alongside current medical students. Like other academic programs, the best special master's programs are competitive and applying early is important. The AAMC has a listing of all special master's programs, and interested applicants should review each program's requirements and when they start accepting applications.

A master's in public health, nutrition, or global health not only can boost students' GPA but will allow them to pursue a specific interest—in and out of the classroom—and improve their overall academic record.

In recent years, more and more "special master's" programs, which are specifically structured to boost a premedical applicant's GPA and candidacy, have been established, including some with osteopathic and Caribbean medical school affiliations. Some programs grant degrees while others do not. In my opinion, if your goal in attending a program is to increase your chances of medical school admission, earning an actual degree is not important and should not influence the decision of whether you should attend a particular program.

How should you decide if a program is worth attending or which program you should attend? I encourage applicants to get as much information about graduates' success as possible when making these important and expensive choices by asking the school specific questions.

How to evaluate a special master's program : What to ask.

• How many students enroll each year?

• How many matriculants finish the program and/ or graduate?

• What percentage of matriculants are accepted to medical school (allopathic, osteopathic, and off-shore)?

• How soon after finishing the program do students typically apply to medical school?

• For students who are not accepted to medical school, what careers do they ultimately pursue?

• You want to attend a special master's program that has a track record of success with the majority (80% or more) of students gaining admission to the type of medical school you hope to attend.

PART 3

APPLYING TO MEDICAL SCHOOL

CHAPTER 9

TMDSAS® AND AACOMAS® MEDICAL SCHOOL APPLICATION SYSTEMS

The major medical school application systems in the United States are: American Medical Colleges Application Service (AMCAS®), Texas Medical and Dental Application Service (TMDSAS®), and American Association of Colleges of Osteopathic Medicine Application Service (AACOMAS®) (See "TMDSAS®, AACOMAS®, and international medical school application tidbits"). International and off-shore medical schools have individual and school-specific applications.

Many medical school applicants apply to medical schools through several application systems simultaneously. The two major parts of the AMCAS application that are in the applicant's control are the personal statement (limit 5,300 characters with spaces) and up to 15 experience descriptions (up to 15 entries that are 700 characters in length with spaces and you can elaborate further on up to three of these 15 experiences using 1,325 characters). While this is not "required," I advise completing "most meaningful" entries and three activities/experiences. Note that these character limits for experience entries represent a change that was instituted starting with the

2012 application. Part 4, the "Composing the Application" portion of this book suggests how applicants can modify their application documents for other application systems.

TMDSAS®

In 2014, the average GPA of TMDSAS® medical school matriculants was 3.72 and the average MCAT® was 30.6

Most Texas medical schools use the TMDSAS® application, which can be submitted in early May (the AMCAS® application is submitted the first week of June), so applicants applying through both AMCAS® and TMDSAS® should submit the Texas application first. The limit for the TMDSAS® personal statement is 5,000 characters and you are allowed only 300 characters for each entry. Given this brevity, most applicants choose to write TMDSAS® entries in a bulleted and "resume style" format. There simply isn't enough space to elaborate about the activity and what you learned from it, as applicants ideally should (and can!) for the AMCAS® entries.

TMDSAS® activities are listed under the following categories:

1. Academic Recognition
2. College Leadership
3. Employment
4. Research Activities
5. Healthcare Activities
6. Community Service
7. Extracurricular and Leisure Activities
8. Planned Activities

Texas requires that applicants account for all time between graduating from high school to the summer of the application.

Texas also has one required shorter essay and two optional essays. These three essays are each limited to 2,500 characters with spaces.

In 2016, the prompt for the first required essay asks applicants to write about personal characteristics.

The second essay is "optional" but applicants are "strongly encouraged to take advantage of this opportunity" so, I would think it wise that applicants complete the essay. The essay asks applicants to provide the admissions committee with a broader picture of who you are.

The final additional essay is truly optional asks applicants to write about any unique circumstances that are not outlined elsewhere in the application.

MCAT®

Unlike with AMCAS®, MCAT® scores are not automatically forwarded to TMDSAS® so applicants must release MCAT® scores on their own.

Match

Texas medical schools also have a match process to gain admission, the results of which are announced annually in February; however, prematch offers can be made in November and December. Only Texas residents can go through a matching process at TMDSAS® medical schools but out of state applicants can apply to Texas medical schools as well through TMDSAS®. Keep in mind that Baylor College of Medicine in Houston, Texas is not part of the TMDSAS® application system. See the TMDSAS® website for further information: http://www.utsystem. edu/tmdsas/medical/homepage.html.

Letters of Reference

For TMDSAS®, unlike AMCAS®, all letters of reference and committee letter packets are mailed directly to the system. Applicants must download a TMDSAS® evaluation form and give a copy to each letter writer. The applicant must sign this form to waive her right to read the letter.

Timeline

The TMDSAS® application is the first of the application systems to allow submission in early May.

Fee

Participation in TMDSAS requires a flat fee of $140.

More Information

For more and the most up-to-date information, visit tmdsas.com.

AACOMAS®

The AACOMAS® personal statement limit is 4,500 characters, and experience descriptions are 750 characters. For the AACOMAS® personal statement, I advise applicants to address why they are specifically interested in osteopathic medicine. Some students like simply to "recycle" their allopathic personal statement for the osteopathic medical school, which I don't advise because of the importance of this inclusion.

However, with 750 characters per application entry, AMCAS® descriptions, which are 700 characters each, can also be used for the osteopathic application. The experience categories in AACOMAS® fall under work, volunteer, community service and extracurricular.

MCAT®

For AACOMAS®, keep in mind that you must request that MCAT® scores be sent to osteopathic medical schools. This will not happen automatically. You can request this via the AAMC website and scores will be transmitted electronically to AACOMAS®.

Letters of Reference

Letters of reference are sent directly to osteopathic medical schools rather than to AACOMAS®. AACOMAS® does not forward letters. This is distinctly different from the other two application services.

Timeline

The timeline for AACOMAS® is similar to that for AMCAS®; the system opens in May and applications can be submitted in early June. For more information: https://aacomas.aacom.org. Early submission is encouraged! After submitting your application, processing can take three to six weeks.

More Information

Fore more information and to get access to the most up to date information, visit aacom.org.

International Medical Schools

Each off-shore and international medical school has its own application. Contact each school individually for details. Essays often ask the applicant to describe his or her interest in medicine but might also require applicants to explain why they are specifically interested in the medical school to which they are applying. These school-specific essays should each be tailored for the individual school.

CHAPTER 10

APPLYING TO MEDICAL SCHOOL AND STAYING ORGANIZED

The key to success in applying to medical school is to stay organized. Some applicants are not successful during their first application cycle not because they don't have the grades, MCAT® score, or experiences to be accepted but because they simply underestimate how much work and time it takes to apply. In the same way that students make strict study plans to prepare for the MCAT®, I suggest that applicants also create a timeline to make sure they do tasks on time. Here is the general list of tasks, in chronologic order, you must complete to apply to medical school:

1. Meet with premed advisor
2. Obtain letters of reference
3. Write application entries
4. Write personal statement
5. Request transcripts
6. Enter biographical and academic record data in the application
7. Complete additional application information (if applicable)
8. Decide where to apply

9. Write secondary essays

AMCAS®, AACOMAS® and TMDSAS® all open in early May, when you can start submitting letters of reference and transcripts and enter all of your application information (see "Working with your premed advisor"). AMCAS® and AACOMAS® allow you to submit your completed application in early June. The AMCAS®, AACOMAS, and TMDSAS instruction manuals are published annually, and you should have one at your side when completing your application. The AMCAS® online application system also has a useful "help" button that you can use as a resource when completing your application. You cannot submit the application itself until the first week of June.

The AMCAS®, AACOMAS®, and TMDSAS® applications are considered the "primary application" and are equivalent to the common application in the college admissions process. The fee to submit an AMCAS® primary application in 2014 was $160 for only one school and $36 for each additional school. After you have submitted the primary application, AMCAS® will begin the verification process, during which it ensures that all courses are listed correctly on the application and that all letter writers "match" what is written in the application. AMCAS® will also calculate your GPAs. Once the verification process is complete, AMCAS® sends the application to the medical schools you have specified. The verification process can take anywhere from 24 hours (this is true) to six weeks, depending on when you submit your application and how well everything "matches." If AMCAS® has any questions about your application, it will contact you.

After medical schools receive your application, they will send you secondary applications. Most schools send secondary applications automatically but some, including the University of California schools, will screen your primary application to determine if you qualify for a secondary application.

Some secondary applications consist simply of forms and a fee request, but most request that you write additional essays and pay a fee ranging from $25 to $100.

Working with your premed advisor

Some undergraduate and postbaccalaureate premed advisors are excellent and experienced while others don't really understand the medical school admissions process and are overwhelmed with the number of students they must help. Nonetheless, if you have a premed advisor who will be responsible for writing your committee letter or sending out your letter packet, you must keep her "in the loop" and involved in your application process, whatever her skill set and insight.

Premed advisors may also advocate for students both on the premedical committee and during the admissions process. Therefore, even if you don't think highly of your premed advisor, you must still be respectful and considerate towards her and be sure she is aware of your plans. Meet with your premed advisor periodically during your undergraduate career because your success will partially depend on her efforts.

CHAPTER 11

AMCAS® APPLICATION COMPONENTS AND CONSIDERATIONS

Every section of the application has its ins and outs and stumbling blocks. Knowing about them in advance can help you with timely submission of letters of reference, transcripts, and the entire medical school application that is necessary to success.

Letters of reference

AMCAS® has a letter of recommendation service that allows letters to be directly uploaded to the AMCAS® system. If you have a prehealth office that is collecting and submitting all of your letters in a "letter packet," you will need to find out who the point of contact is in the prehealth office and list this person as your only letter writer "contact" in the letters of evaluation/recommendation section of the AMCAS® application. You must download a form from AMCAS® so this person can then upload your letter packet.

If you are asking each individual letter writer to submit his and her letter to AMCAS®, you will need to download a letter submission form for each person and list each of these individuals as "primary authors" in the letters of evaluation/recommendation section of the AMCAS® application.

If you want a particular individual letter sent only to certain schools, the AMCAS ® application gives you the flexibility to do so. Each letter you list can be "assigned" to specific schools so not every letter must be sent to every school.

You are allowed to submit up to 10 letters of reference via AMCAS®, and a letter packet is considered only one letter (See "What is a letter packet?"). (You can mail your letters directly to AMCAS®, but if you choose this option, be sure to follow up to ensure that AMCAS® received your letters.) For more information on the AMCAS® letters of evaluation/recommendation service visit: https://www.aamc.org/students/applying/amcas/faqs/63226/faq_amcasletters.html.

Students who don't have a prehealth office and want a safe way to "store" letters for a short period of time before they apply can use services that will collect these letters and then "deliver" them to AMCAS® or any other destination. These services are Interfolio (interfolio.com) and VirtualEvals (virtualevals.com).

What is a letter packet?

Undergraduate colleges and some postbaccalaureate programs have premedical committees and advisors that will collect all of your letters and submit them in a "packet." When indicating on the AMCAS® application who will be submitting your letters, you indicate only the designated contact in the premedical office who is responsible for submitting your packet.

Transcripts

Transcript discrepancies are a primary cause of AMCAS® verification delays. AMCAS® requires that students submit official transcripts from every US, Canadian, and US territorial school where they completed or attempted course work—even if they didn't earn any credit. You should download a transcript request form for every school at which you took classes and send or take the form to each registrar and request that a transcript be sent to AMCAS®. You are required to list all courses you have taken even if you withdrew, failed, or repeated a course. Even if your school "erased" a course from your transcript because of a forgiveness policy, you are still required to enter this course work in the application. If credits were transferred from another college to your college, the transcript from the school where courses were originally taken must be provided. Credits earned in study abroad programs, if sponsored by a US, Canadian, or US territorial colleges, may qualify for transcript exemptions, with transcripts from the foreign college not needed. You must list courses taken abroad exactly as they appear on your official transcript from the institution that sponsored the study abroad program. For further information about how specific course work should be listed, including "repeat courses" and foreign and study abroad course work, contact your college registrar or refer to the AMCAS® instruction manual, which is published annually. It is also wise to have copies of official transcripts for your own use so you can complete the course work section of the application accurately. After AMCAS® receives official transcripts, it will send and email receipt.

AMCAS® sections

The following are the sections of the AMCAS® application in the order in which they are listed. Because reviewers generally read the application in this order, it's wise to be aware of it as you compose your application. For example, by the time the reviewer reads your personal statement— the last but important section of the application—he already knows about your biographic and academic background and the activities in which you have been involved. Knowing this may influence how you write about a specific experience in your personal statement and your decision about whether to explain "red flags" in it. (Occasionally, a reviewer has a personal preference for an order that deviates from the norm.)

Be sure to fill out every section of the AMCAS® application except those sections that don't apply to you (see "Your email address: Its importance and your image").

1. Identifying Information
2. Colleges Attended
3. Previous Medical School Matriculation (if applicable)
4. Institutional Action (if applicable)
5. Biographic Information and Childhood Information
6. Disadvantaged Status (if applicable)
7. Felony (if applicable)
8. Academic Record (all course work, grades, and hours)
9. Verified Grade Point Averages (AMCAS ®calculates your GPAs)
10. Experiences Section (Activities)
11. Letters of Evaluation
12. Medical School Designations
13. Personal Comments (usually referred to as the "Personal Statement") and MD/PhD Essay and

Research Essay (MD/PhD and Research essay are for MD/PhD applicants only)

14. MCAT® Test Scores
15. Other test scores (GRE, or anything else you choose to list)
16. Certification and Submission

Your email address: Its importance and your image

The primary way that AMCAS® and medical schools communicate with you is via email. You therefore should assign one email address for listing on your application and check it frequently. Because students now are so "text" focused, all too often some of them forget to check email and miss important messages. Your email address often gives admissions officers (and the other committee members) their first impression of you. Just as your style of dress on interview day conveys a sense of your professionalism and maturity, your email address says a lot about you as well. When I was an admissions officer, some applicants' email addresses made me pause and question their judgment. It is best to keep your email address simple and professional. I suggest using an email address that has some variation of your first and last name.

School "deadlines"

I recommend that you consider "opening dates" of application systems as deadlines. Applicants rarely are accepted to medical school if they wait for primary or secondary application submission deadlines, and I therefore encourage all applicants to ignore official deadlines. That said, for the record, primary application deadlines range from October 1st to December 15th depending on the individual medical school, each of which independently determines deadlines. (see "The importance of submitting an early application")

The importance of submitting an early application

Since most medical schools extend interviews on a rolling basis, it is extremely important to submit your medical school application as close to the opening date of the system as possible (for AMCAS® this opening date is in the first few days of June). Also be aware that AMCAS® won't verify your application until it receives all documentation. Application processing and verification can take up to six weeks, but if you submit early this processing often takes much less time. Keep in mind that the AMCAS® application system can be accessed in early May and, at this time, you can enter all of your application information (including activities entries and essays), request transcripts, and have letters of reference sent to AMCAS®.

You should also submit secondary applications and essays soon after you receive requests for them. I suggest that you "turn around" secondary applications and essays within two weeks.

Taking a "late" MCAT® can also delay review of your application since most medical schools will not review an application until they have received all pending exam scores. This is why it is wise to take the MCAT® by no later than June of the year you plan to apply.

Fee assistance program

Applicants who do not have the financial resources to take the MCAT® and apply to medical school can apply for the fee assistance program (FAP). Applicants must apply for the FAP in the year that they plan to take the MCAT®; the application opens in January of each year and applicants should apply as early as possible. The FAP reduces the MCAT® fee to $100, and students may apply to up to 14 schools without a fee. For more information about this program, eligibility requirements, and application instructions, see: https://www.aamc.org/students/applying/fap/.

CHAPTER 12

WHERE SHOULD I APPLY?

Students often are overwhelmed when deciding where to apply. Some students are excessively concerned with official medical school rankings, which I discourage. Looking closely at what each medical school offers and how its graduates perform is most important in determining the best choices for you.

Deciding where to apply should be based on several factors:

1. How well can you compete with other applicants?

To determine your competitive position as an applicant, consider your GPA and MCAT® scores. You should review the statistics for matriculated or accepted applicants at all medical schools to determine where to apply. This information can be found in the Medical School Admissions Requirements (MSAR®) book published and available in an online version from the AAMC® and in the online premium edition of US News and World Report. That report also lists the number of applicants who are interviewed and accepted and therefore provides more data than the most recent MSAR® edition that was published when this book was written (http://grad-schools.usnews.rankingsandreviews.com/best-graduate-schools)

2. What are your geographic preferences?

Many students prefer to attend medical school in a particular area of the country. Also keep in mind that many students end up doing their residency training where they attended medical school or at their medical school's affiliated hospitals. Applicants who are very competitive can sometimes have the luxury of choosing where they would like to attend school; however, those who are less competitive often cannot be this choosy.

3. How do you learn best?

Some medical school curriculums still consist of lectures and labs as primary teaching methods, but most have now moved towards small group, case based learning, which is also referred to as problem based learning (PBL). PBL encourages collaborative problem solving and peer education. Almost all schools now incorporate into their curriculums simulation learning, where students work on computerized mannequins to help them learn to diagnose and treat patients. Some schools have more sophisticated "sim centers" than others but don't be fooled; effective learning requires outstanding teachers and supportive educational environments, which does not always correlate with impressive facilities. Prestigious medical schools typically have the most progressive curriculums, and many medical schools are now incorporating "longitudinal patient care experiences" through which medical students care for the same patients during a specified period.

The trend in undergraduate medical education is to blur the line between the preclinical (first and second years) and clinical years (third and fourth years) of medical school, a distinction that used to be well defined. This blurring is being accomplished by incorporating varying degrees of early patient exposure in medical schools throughout the country. Though I discourage students from considering curriculums in deciding where they should apply, variations in curriculums can be factored in if you have to choose between multiple medical schools. Also consider that most of your last two years are spent doing rotations at hospitals affiliated with the medical school you attend. Consider these environments, too, as you decide where to apply.

4. Do you have financial considerations?

Medical school is expensive, and some students prefer to attend an in-state medical school to defray costs. Some medical schools also have large endowments and offer generous scholarships to some accepted applicants.

5. Do you have any special interests that you want to pursue during medical school?

Most outstanding medical schools have excellent departments in most disciplines, but if you have a special interest in a particular field, be aware of what medical schools have programs that will allow you to explore and develop your niche. If you know you want to practice primary care in a community setting and have no interest in research, for example, attending a medical school with a research requirement where most students go on to subspecialize might be a poor choice.

6. Grading systems

Medical schools have different grading systems; some are pass/fail, others are fail/pass/high pass/honors, while others offer letter grades. Pass/fail environments tend to be less competitive and more collaborative (for obvious reasons), and pass/fail grading systems are typically in place at the more competitive medical schools. If you have a strong idea of what grading system you prefer, it is better to factor this into your decision after you are accepted.

7. How do the medical school's students fare in the residency match?

Reviewing a medical school's residency match list will tell you in what specialties and where students match to complete their residency training. The match process, conducted by the National Residency Matching Program® (NRMP®), for most specialties and the SF Match® for a few, is too complex to review in detail here, but put simply, medical students interview at residency programs and then rank those programs in order of preference. Residency programs also rank all applicants in their preference order. Then annually in mid-March, students and programs find out their match results. The match algorithm works in favor of the applicant, and medical schools will often boast what percentage of students "got one of their top three match preferences."

Interpreting a medical school's residency match data is not always easy for a medical school applicant. For example, if a medical school graduates many students who practice primary care, it is not likely to have as many "competitive specialty matches" as a school whose graduates gravitate towards specialty practice.

In general, however, the more competitive the medical school, the higher percentage of residency matches the school will have in the most competitive specialties (see "Competitive residency matches"). Be aware, though, that within each specialty some residency programs might be very competitive; the catch is that without being a part of that specialty it is tough to know what those top residency programs are.

Competitive residency matches

Dermatology
Neurological surgery
Otolaryngology
Orthopaedic surgery
Ophthalmology
Plastic surgery
Radiation oncology

Another way to objectively evaluate a medical school's success is to review graduates' average United States Licensing Exam (USMLE®) results, specifically the USMLE® Step 1. Medical students take the USMLE® Step 1 at the end of the second year of medical school and take USMLE® Step 2 (USMLE® Step 2 has two parts – clinical knowledge and clinical skills), during their fourth year of medical school.

8. Is the medical school's mission aligned with your ideals?

To learn what a school values, always review a medical school's mission statement before you apply. Though most mission statements are similar and emphasize the importance of education, research, and community service, some schools place more importance on certain areas, such as primary care, rural medicine, and research, which is not reflected in their statement. So look beyond a school's mission statement to ensure that their focus matches your interests and goals by reading the fine print on the medical school's website, and also review the website of the medical school's affiliated hospitals so you know in what clinical areas the hospital excels.

9. To how many schools should I apply?

If you are a very competitive applicant (high GPA, MCAT®, and impressive achievements), you may need to apply to only 15 schools. However, I typically recommend that applicants apply to at least 20 schools and for those who don't have "over the top stats," submitting 25 to 30 applications is more likely to yield more interview invitations than a smaller number of applications (see "State schools: Sometimes a good choice"). Applying broadly is also important. A "safety" medical school simply doesn't exist and even if you are an above average to outstanding applicant, you must apply to a wide range of schools based on average MCAT® score and GPAs of accepted applicants. Since the admissions process includes a great deal of subjectivity, casting a wide net and applying broadly is always a good idea to improve your chances of being accepted.

Early decision?

I recommend applying early decision to a medical school only if you are an outstanding applicant and fairly confident that you will be accepted to that school. Here's why: If you aren't accepted, your early decision medical school will notify you in October when you can then apply to other schools. But your applications to these other schools will then be late relative to other applicants, which decreases your chances of admission.

State schools: Sometimes a good choice

In general, state schools tend to be less competitive than private schools, as long as you reside in that state. If you are unsure of which state considers you a resident, contact the school or the state's governmental offices for residency requirements.

Some state schools also accept a large number of out-of-state applicants. A state school whose out-of-state students represent 25% or more of matriculants is a good bet for the out-of-state applicant.

CHAPTER 13

OSTEOPATHIC MEDICAL SCHOOLS

Your decision to apply to osteopathic medical schools should be based on whether or not you can achieve your goals by doing so. The reality is that many physicians, regardless of where they are educated, practice medicine in the same way, in the same settings, and in the same specialties. Many people can achieve their goals by graduating from osteopathic or off-shore medical schools. With 37 osteopathic medical schools in the United States and total enrollments of just over 6,500 first year students, more and more applicants are opting for osteopathic medical educations.

What are the similarities between an allopathic and osteopathic medical education?

The fundamental education students receive is very similar. At both osteopathic and allopathic medical schools, students learn about anatomy, histology, and physiology to name a few areas of study. Typically, the first two years are dominated by classroom, small group, and laboratory and medical simulation learning. The third and fourth years of medical school consist of clinical rotations. The third year comprises mostly "core" rotations such as pediatrics, medicine, and surgery and the fourth year often offers some greater flexibility for elective course work.

The most obvious distinction between allopathic and osteopathic medical schools is that graduates of allopathic medical schools earn a medical doctor degree (or M.D.) whereas osteopathic graduates earn a doctor of osteopathic medicine degree (or D.O.). So, simply looking at the initials next to a doctor's name will tell you what type of medical school he or she attended.

The other significant way in which osteopathic and allopathic medical educations differ is that osteopathic medical students, starting very early in their medical educations, learn osteopathic manipulative medicine (OMM) of the spine, bones, and muscles as an adjunct to diagnosing and treating patients. Students spend about 200 hours of their osteopathic medical educations learning about OMM. In addition, at least in theory, osteopathic education puts a greater emphasis on the importance of holistic care, which highlights the value of getting to know one's patients as people and carefully considering the value of preventive care and patient education. In my experience, however, allopathic medical schools espouse similar ideals.

Is it competitive to get into osteopathic medical schools?

For most applicants the answer to this question is "yes" ; getting accepted to an osteopathic school isn't easy— one must still do very well in medical school prerequisites and on the MCAT® and must pursue meaningful extracurricular activities. The competition for admission is intense. Last year, nearly 16,500 applicants competed for 6,400 first year spots. The osteopathic medical students who started in 2014, for example, had an average MCAT® of 27 and an overall GPA of 3.5. This compares with an average MCAT® of 31.4 and overall GPA of 3.7 for allopathic students who matriculated last year. The Osteopathic Medical College Information Book is an excellent resource to help determine which osteopathic school may be a good fit for you. Here is the link: www. aacom.org/news-and-events/publications/cib_final.

What do osteopathic physicians practice and what are my chances of getting the residency I want?

More than 50% of osteopathic medical school graduates, who may continue their training in allopathic or osteopathic residency programs, practice in areas of primary care, including family practice, internal medicine, and pediatrics. This high percentage is because osteopathic medical schools attract students who are interested in primary care. Starting next year, the Accreditation Council of Graduate Medical Education, the accreditation body for allopathic residency programs, will start to accredit osteopathic programs, too. This will ensure that training standards are the same for allopathic and osteopathic residency programs.

COMLEX or USMLE— which licensure exam do I take?

When applying to osteopathic medical school, it is important to understand the difference between these two licensing exams. The COMLEX, or comprehensive osteopathic medical licensure exam, is the preferred exam for osteopathic residency admissions committees. The United States Licensing Exam, or USMLE, is the preferred exam of allopathic residency programs. Osteopathic medical school students can increase their residency training opportunities by taking both exams, which allows them to be competitive for both osteopathic and allopathic residency programs.

One of my osteopathic medical school clients, for example,

decided to play it safe and take both the COMLEX and USMLE exams and applied to both osteopathic and allopathic residency programs. She recently matched into a competitive allopathic emergency medicine residency.

Should I apply to osteopathic medical schools?

In making this decision, you must understand the nuances of osteopathic practice. The best way to do this is to shadow an osteopathic physician and talk with osteopathic physicians about how they practice. In my experience, the way in which osteopathic and allopathic physicians practice varies little. Nonetheless, many highly competitive allopathic residency programs will consider only allopathic medical school graduates. With this in mind, you should consider which specialties you might want to pursue before setting your sights on an osteopathic medical school. Keep in mind that many osteopathic physicians are successful and productive practitioners and offer excellent medical care.

PART 4

COMPOSING THE MEDICAL SCHOOL APPLICATION

CHAPTER 14

MEDICAL SCHOOL APPLICATION BASICS

The medical school application consists of all documents to which medical schools have access, including transcripts and letters of reference. The applicant has control over some of these documents, namely application entries, personal statement, secondary essays and, for some, background and institutional action descriptions (see "Composing your application: What to keep in mind"). I encourage students to start composing their application materials in the winter of the year they plan to apply. Creating excellent written documents takes time, and the longer you have to consider what is important to you, the better your documents will be.

Composing your application: What to keep in mind

Create written materials that demonstrate insight, introspection, and lessons learned.

Make sure your materials provide evidence that you have the qualities and characteristics medical schools are looking for (listed in Chapter 5). Keep in mind that unlike for your college application, you don't want to try to stand out by writing about your artistic or athletic accomplishments in your personal statement. You also don't want to be overly creative. While medical schools respect and consider unique approaches and significant accomplishments, the "hook" that got you into college won't necessarily help you gain admission to medical school unless that "hook" was medically or scientifically related.

Content is more important than writing skill.

Medical school admissions committees are not looking for the next literary prize winner and will not examine your written work with a fine-tooth comb. While you should take pains to avoid obvious errors, submitting an essay fit for publication could even seem suspect unless you have a writing background. Medical school admissions committees are most concerned with your overall message and meaning, and submitting materials that are over-edited or beyond your verbal abilities might do more harm than good because your actual abilities could become evident during interviews.

Be specific.

Aim to give your application broad appeal, keeping in mind that every reviewer has an individual personal bias, level of experience, and specialty or medical focus, as well as his or her own ideas of what to look for in an application.

Make sure your application entries and personal statement complement each other. The reviewer will read your application entries and personal statement one after the other. Be sure that your personal statement is fresh and doesn't just repeat what you have written in your application entries.

Don't leave out informal shadowing or other valuable experiences, even if they are not part of a formal program. Applicants sometimes fall short in the area of clinical exposure because they think the application entries are only for formal programs or projects.

Concentrate on showing depth and breadth rather than superficial involvements. Don't try to "fill the space"; listing one-day experiences just to fill out the application, for example, may dilute an otherwise substantial application. Though you are allowed 15 experience entries, if you write about only nine quality experiences you follow a long line of successful medical students who did the same.

Merge activity entries, if necessary.

If you have too many experiences to describe in the allotted space, choose those that are significant enough to list and then figure out how to merge entries creatively. (See how Amy did this successfully in the sample application in chapter 22.)

Even though many people incorporate anecdotes in their materials, don't take this approach if it doesn't feel comfortable or doesn't suit your style. I still encourage applicants to have an experience-based essay, but it is perfectly acceptable if you write a first-person narrative explaining how your experiences have influenced you and why.

Allow time for multiple revisions.

You can't do good work when you rush. Check your spelling and grammar, and be sure the document has no typos! Copy and paste your documents from a text editor to the application itself to avoid formatting errors. **Always proofread your entire application before submitting. After submitting, check the status of your application often.**

Applying through multiple systems

If you are also submitting an application via TMDSAS®, I suggest first writing the AMCAS® personal statement and then cutting characters (if necessary) to meet the 5,000 character limit imposed by TMDSAS®. Since activity descriptions for TMDSAS® are brief (fewer than 300 characters), these entries should be matter of fact without embellishment or anecdote.

If you are applying for AACOMAS® in addition to AMCAS®, I suggest writing a new personal statement although you can likely use portions of the AMCAS® personal statement. Since the character limit for AACOMAS® is only 4,500 characters and you must also explain your specific interest in osteopathic medicine, using your AMCAS® personal statement would not be wise. **AMCAS® experience entries have character limits of 700 so these writeups can also be used for AACOMAS®.**

CHAPTER 15

WHO IS YOUR AUDIENCE?

Whenever you write a document, a letter, or an email, or prepare for a presentation or interview, you first consider your audience. The same is true of medical school applications; you must consider who will be reading the document you are preparing. If you are like most applicants, you will be applying to a wide range of schools in a variety of geographic areas. The primary AMCAS® application, similar to the common application for college, will be reviewed by all medical schools to which you apply. The disposition, background, medical specialty, and level of experience of your reviewers will vary.

At one school, a basic science professor will review your application, while at another a physician who has worked in medical education for years will review your work; at a third institution, a physician who has recently retired from clinical medicine will review your application, while at another a fourth year medical student will primarily be responsible for deciding if you will be invited for an interview.

Some realistic (but somewhat surprising) scenarios

- The basic science PhD may or may not understand what medical schools are looking for in applicants today. He or she may be more focused on subjects with which he is familiar, namely basic science research. He may think that if an applicant doesn't have significant research in her background she is not a worthy candidate.

- A recently retired physician may have plenty of experience but, depending on how up to date the physician is with trends in medical admissions, he may still be making decisions based on an old framework of what the medical school is seeking in an applicant. He may also have extra time on his hands and serves on the admissions committee to remain involved, and may therefore read every document in your entire application, and take notes.

- A medical student reviewer may read every word of your application (students tend to be very careful). The student also has limited experience, of course, and will naturally compare his own application with yours. Medical students tend to make admissions decisions that are less objective and more emotionally and subjectively founded than other reviewers.

- A current medical educator is experienced and tends to be open minded and up to date on what his medical school and medical schools around the country are seeking. He will generally apply few biases when reviewing applications. He also may not feel the need to review your application as thoroughly as someone with less experience since he probably can quickly identify if you have the academic and personal attributes the school wants in applicants it invites for an interview.

The smaller the admissions committee and the fewer interview invitations it offers, the more likely that your application will be reviewed by an experienced medical educator. However, since most medical schools manually review huge numbers of applications, not enough experienced individuals are available to read all of them and, as a result, many (relatively) inexperienced people make screening decisions.

Even though most medical schools have checklists or grading systems for reviewers to use when deciding whether to interview an applicant, you can see that your main goal when you compose your application is to try and have broad appeal. You have no way of modifying the answers or style of your documents to suit your reviewer. This is why applications must be interesting and appealing overall so every reviewer can find something that resonates with what he or she is seeking.

CHAPTER 16

APPLICATION AND "MOST MEANINGFUL" EXPERIENCES/ACTIVITIES

The AMCAS® application offers the opportunity to write about up to 15 experience descriptions that are up to 700 characters in length. Applicants then select up to three (and at least one if you have a minimum of two experience descriptions) of these 15 that they consider their "most meaningful experiences" and can use up to1,325 characters (including spaces, hard returns count as two spaces) to elaborate on why the experience was meaningful. For each experience, applicants select one of the categories AMCAS® specifies (see "AMCAS® activities entries categories"). You also need to write out a specific experience name, contact name and title, organization name, city, state, and country of the activity, dates of the activity, and average hours per week. **The AMCAS® system automatically lists the activities in chronologic order with the most recent activity first.**

AMCAS® activities entries categories

Research/Lab
Teaching/Tutoring

Community Service/Volunteer – Not Medical/
Clinical
Community Service/Volunteer – Medical/Clinical
Paid Employment – Not Military
Paid Employment – Military
Publications
Conferences Attended
Presentations/Posters
Honors/Awards/Recognitions
Extracurricular/Hobbies/Avocations
Leadership – Not listed elsewhere
Other

AMCAS® Tidbits

1. Childhood Information: All applicants must complete a "childhood section" where they enter information about family income, family need for federal or state assistance, applicant work history and contribution to family income, and information about how applicants paid for post-secondary education. In the past, only applicants who considered themselves disadvantaged had to complete this information.

2. Work/Activities Entries: Applicants can write about up to 15 experiences in 700 characters or less. Applicants *must* then select *up to three* of these experiences that they consider the "most meaningful" and elaborate on those three activities using up to 1,325 characters. To clarify, the three experiences you choose as "most meaningful" have two parts: One is 700 characters and describes the activity, and one is 1,325 characters, which

allows you to elaborate on why this experience was significant. In the application, the 700 character description appears first, immediately followed by the 1,325 character elaboration. AMCAS® automatically puts all entries, whether "most meaningful" or not, in chronologic order.

3. Certification and Submission Language: Applicants must certify, in addition to other items, that, "all written passages, such as the personal statement, essays required from MD/PhD applicants and descriptions of work/activities, are my own and have not been written, in part or in whole, by a third party." As mentioned elsewhere in this book, be careful when selecting who will "edit" your essay. Having someone "overedit" or ghostwrite your work is not only immoral but can jeopardize your success; if who you are on paper doesn't match who you are in person, your interviewer may sense something fishy.

Always check the most up to date AMCAS® instructions before you fill out the application because AMCAS® can alter them for any given year.

Experience Entries

Medical schools place great emphasis on evaluating candidates' "personal competencies," and I can tell you from experience that applicants who write fully about the experiences that had the greatest influence on them and their path to medicine have an advantage in the application process. Reviewers are looking for compelling evidence that you are worthy of an interview invitation, and activities descriptions, especially for an applicant who doesn't have "over the top stats," can make or break this decision.

In fact, a few schools openly state that they now place greater emphasis on the activities descriptions than on the personal statement. You should devote as much time to composing your experience descriptions as you do to writing your personal statement. And keep in mind that reviewers typically read your activities descriptions before your personal statement since this is the predetermined order of the application. You want them to read your statement with a "good impression" of who you are based on what they have already read. This "halo effect" will then influence the way they interpret your personal statement, increasing your chances of being invited for an interview.

Do not be concerned if you don't have an experience for each category. As mentioned elsewhere in this book, medical schools would much rather see that students have sought out meaningful and long term experiences in a few areas rather than multiple, superficial experiences in many different areas.

AMCAS® allows students to write descriptions of up to 15 experiences in only 700 characters. For these entries, applicants must be brief and to the point, but I still encourage a narrative approach. Consider the person reviewing your application; do you think she would rather read bullet points or a descriptive explanation about your responsibilities and experience? Indeed, you may have a reviewer who is rushed and might simply skim your application, but let him make the choice if he wants to read less. With only 700 characters, you don't have much room for introspection, but you still can add some insights if you have the space after explaining your activity. When possible, try to demonstrate "results" for your experiences. For example, if you worked on a fundraiser, mention how much money you raised. If you were the leader of a club, organization, or group, mention by how much membership grew while you were in charge.

Most meaningful experience entries

AMCAS® requests that applicants select up to three experiences that they consider "most meaningful" and offer applicants the chance to write about these experiences in depth (up to 1,325 characters with spaces for each of the three experiences). If you write two or more "regular" experience entries, you are required by AMCAS® to choose at least one that is "most meaningful." I advise applicants to write all three "most meaningful" summaries, however. To be clear, applicants write a 700 character description of each activity and then choose up to three of these experiences upon which to elaborate. Therefore, for each of those activities that applicants choose as "most meaningful," they write two descriptions: One 700 character description describes the activity, and one 1,325 character description, which is placed directly beneath the shorter description, discusses why this experience was meaningful.

As you write about these three activities, think not only about what you did during that activity but what it meant to you, what you learned, and how it influenced your path and choices. You should also write about how the meaningful experience influenced your ideals, insights, perspectives, and goals. Medical school admissions committees use your application to evaluate your personal characteristics (see box in Chapter 4), and the best applications demonstrate passion, enthusiasm, insight, and introspection. Committees also want to be convinced of your commitment to and understanding of the practice of medicine. Your participation in activities should not be superficial, which gives the impression that you take on activities just for the sake of doing so. Particularly for the three experiences you choose to describe more fully, demonstrate that your involvement is deep and that you actually learned something from your participation. (see, "Meaningful experiences: Which should I choose?")

Meaningful experiences: Which should I choose?

Deciding which experiences have been most meaningful to you is entirely personal and depends on several factors. When it comes to experiences, applicants typically fall into one of two categories: 1) They have had multiple meaningful experiences and cannot decide about which to elaborate or 2) They have had only a few meaningful experiences and worry they don't have enough experiences to write about. If you are in the first category, it is best to first decide which experiences you will highlight in your personal statement. Ideally, you should then write about your other meaningful experiences as your "most meaningful" experience entries. Applicants who have had fewer meaningful experiences are in a more difficult position. These applicants may be forced to write about the same experiences in both their personal statement and as their "most meaningful" experience entries. They then face the challenge of writing about different aspects of the experience in the two documents and avoiding use of the same turns of phrase.

Ideally, two of your "most meaningful" experiences should be related to medicine, volunteerism/ community service, science, research, clinical experiences, or teaching. It would seem suspect, for example, if your three "most meaningful" entries were about extracurricular hobbies or activities that had nothing to do with endeavors that medical school admissions committees value most.

How do I list titles and contacts in my entry headings?

Try to enter titles, contact names, and hours as accurately as possible. Give the activity a descriptive title and choose a logical category. You won't necessarily have a contact for every activity, which is okay. If the activity you describe, such as a hobby, does not have a contact name, write NA (not applicable). Approximate the hours worked, which may have varied over the course of your involvement in any given activity. As with everything in your application, be as honest and accurate as possible. If you participated in one activity every other week for five hours over the course of two years, then state that in the description of the activity. Only in extreme cases does anyone actually call a contact or verify your involvement. That said, never lie or write something that isn't true and don't overembellish. If, for example, you worked in a lab and spent your summer only pipetting and entering data in a computer, then say so. But, to enhance the entry, you could also write that this experience provided the foundation for a laboratory experience you had later on in which you did have greater responsibility.

How do I list the hours I spent on each activity?

AMCAS® allows you to enter the total time you spent on an activity. The maximum amount of hours you can enter is 999. So, let's say you spent a total of 2,000 hours in a research project over three years totaling 2,000 hours? The maximum number of hours you can enter is 999.

Admissions committees realize this is the limit and will understand that you actually spent more time than that on the activity. I advise applicants not to be too concerned with hours. But be honest when totaling the number of hours spent on each activity.

CHAPTER 17

MEDICAL SCHOOL PERSONAL STATEMENT CONTENT

Your personal statement needs to communicate the following effectively:

- Your interest in medicine
- Your commitment to medicine
- What motivated you to pursue a career in medicine
- What distinguishes you from other candidates
- Special hardships or circumstances that are not explained elsewhere in your application

Your personal statement is where you should write about any pivotal experiences that have influenced your decision to pursue a career in medicine. **Not everyone has had a life-changing or pivotal experience and that is okay. Every year medical schools accept many applicants because they worked hard, earned good grades, and were involved in meaningful activities.** Some applicants' interest in medicine evolved from an interest in science or the human body, which led to the pursuit of activities to explore these interests. For others, however, a life event sparked or confirmed their desire to learn more about a medical career.

Many people's pivotal experiences fall into the following categories:

- Personal experience with illness
- A loved one was sick or died
- Parent or family member was a doctor
- Hardship (family, personal, financial, medical)
- Lack of fulfillment in another academic discipline/ career/job that made them seek out other career options

These pivotal experiences and motivations may be common among applicants, but the observations and the flow of experiences are unique for each individual. Sometimes these pivotal experiences might seem trite or commonplace, but you can write about them creatively.

Don't shy away from writing about your most personal experiences if you are comfortable with doing so. I have seen effective personal statements that have included discussions about such personal topics as depression, illness, personal or family struggles, and coming out. As long as these pivotal experiences are presented as motivating experiences and you explain why they are motivating, you won't sound like a "whiner," a "sobber," or a negative person. Some people might advise you never to write about such sensitive topics, but if you show what you learned from each experience, how that experience helped you to grow, how it made you a better person, and how it will make you a better doctor, you are likely to win over admissions officers. I do, however, discourage students from discussing in written documents learning disabilities or major psychiatric disorders. Even though there are many successful doctors who have learning disabilities, admissions officers are still generally uncomfortable with this topic so it is best to avoid it. Psychiatric disorders can also make admissions officers nervous. (Depression is an exception because it is so common and can often be situational.) It is also unwise to write about how a bad breakup or relationship was especially influential in deciding on a medical career.

CHAPTER 18

PERSONAL STATEMENT BRAINSTORMING AND WRITING

When composing your personal statement, keep in mind that you are writing, in effect, a "story" of how you arrived at this point in your life. But, unlike a "story" in the creative sense, yours must also offer convincing evidence for your decision to apply to medical school. Before starting your personal statement, create an experience-based personal inventory:

1. Write down a list of the most important experiences in your life and your development. The list should be all inclusive and comprise those experiences that had the most impact on you. Put the list, which should consist of personal, extracurricular, and academic events, in chronologic order. From this list, determine which experiences you consider the most important in helping you decide to pursue a career in medicine. This "experience oriented" approach will allow you to determine which experiences best illustrate the personal competencies admissions committees look for in your written documents. Remember that you must provide evidence for your interest in medicine

and for most of the personal qualities and characteristics that medical school admissions committees want to see.

2. After making your list, think about why each "most important" experience was influential and write that down. What did you observe? What did you learn? What insights did you gain? How did the experience influence your path and choices?

3. Then think of a story or illustration for why each experience was important.

4. After doing this exercise, evaluate each experience for its significance and influence and for its "story" value. Choose to write about those experiences that not only were influential but that also will provide interesting reading, keeping in mind that your goal is to weave the pertinent experiences together into a compelling story. In making your choices, think about how you will link each experience and transition from one topic to the next.

5. Decide which of your listed experiences you will use for your personal statement and create a general outline.

6. Start writing.

7. Revise (repeat as many times necessary).

8. Have someone read your work.

Having someone read and evaluate your work is always important. Consider asking your premedical advisor, a professor, a family member, or a friend to review your statement. But be careful not to have too many people read your documents because everyone you ask will feel impelled to give you their "two cents," and too many opinions can make you anxious and delay completion of the documents in a timely fashion. For the same reason, make sure not to ask for opinions too close to your submission date. For example, if you value the opinion of your friend, your uncle, your professor, your mother, and your premed advisor, get all of their opinions early in the process. But by the time you are nearly done with your statement, I suggest having only one or two "go to" people for opinions.

CHAPTER 19

PERSONAL STATEMENT STRUCTURE

AMCAS® allows you 5,300 characters (with spaces, and hard returns count as two spaces) to write your personal statement. Do not feel you must "max out" the space. I have read beautiful and effective personal statements that are only 3,500 characters but generally recommend that your statement be at least 4,300 characters.

A great introduction

Your personal statement should be descriptive, interesting, and compelling (see "Personal statement basics"). Most important is to begin with something that engages your reader. A narrative, a "story," an anecdote written in the first or third person, is ideal. Whatever your approach, your first paragraph must grab your reader's attention and motivate him to want to continue reading. I encourage applicants to start their personal statement by describing an experience that was especially influential in setting them on their path to medical school. This can be a personal experience or an extracurricular one. In general, it is best to "show" rather than "tell" in your introduction as well as in the rest of your essay. How to do this will become clearer as you read examples of personal statements in this book. Remember to avoid clichés and quotes and to be honest and authentic in your writing. Don't try to be someone whom you are not or "tell them what you think they want to hear"; consistency is key and your interviewer is going to make sure that you are who you say you are!

Personal statement basics

1. *Compose a compelling introduction.* Grabbing your reader's attention in the first sentence and paragraph of your statement is key. Even though many applicants use anecdotes, don't take this approach if it doesn't feel comfortable or doesn't suit your style. Just be sure to explain how your experiences have influenced you and why.

2. *Focus the essay on your interest in medicine.* Don't write an entire essay about a hobby or talent.

3. *Do not use quotes or clichés:* This statement should be about you. Using quotes from a famous individual or overly familiar phrases discredits you.

4. *Don't use the personal statement to write about your knowledge of medicine.* Sometimes students use their essay as almost a soap box to write about their viewpoints, or "what the practice of medicine is." This is not the purpose of the essay.

5. *Don't explain why you aren't interested in other professions or write anything negative about another profession.* If you are a career changer, you should mention what was "missing" in

the profession you are leaving but avoid bad-mouthing it.

6. *Make your personal statement authentic, honest, and, as the title suggests, personal.*

7. *Be sure your personal statement flows.* Personal statements for medical school rarely have a theme or thesis. What is important is that your essay flows and makes logical sense. This requires good paragraph transitions.

8. *Don't write about every applicable experience in your statement.* Not only is this impossible, but it is unnecessary because reviewers typically read your application entries before your statement and consider both these pieces of the application together. In fact, you should try to minimize overlap between your application entries and your statement; when your statement themes make it appropriate to repeat an experience already addressed in your application entries, try to take a different approach or at least to use different words in describing the experience in your statement.

9. *Never write about any topic that you would make you uncomfortable if an interviewer wants to discuss it.*

10. *Use active voice.* For example:
The medical center already has implemented these suggestions.

NOT

These suggestions already have been implemented by the medical center.

11. *Avoid weak constructions like "there is," "there are," or "it is."* For example:

    Studying hard is important.

    NOT

    It is important to study hard.

12. *Try not to repeat the same words within one sentence or two adjacent sentences and avoid multisyllabic words*—except to introduce variety—when a simpler word will do as well—. For example:

13. "About" NOT "approximately"; "use" NOT "utilize"; "shows" NOT "exemplifies"

14. *Don't get hung up on health care vs healthcare or multi-factorial vs multifactorial and other such stylistic choices, but do try for spelling consistency in your documents.*

15. *Check grammar and spelling.* This may be obvious, but can't be repeated too often.

    Note: Many grammar/style books are available, but we recommend *The Elements of Style* by William Strunk and E.B. White. It's wise, concise, and fun to read. We do not suggest using editing software, which can often suggest changes that are wrong and cannot mimic the skill of good writers and editors.

The body of the essay

You must decide which experiences, either personal or extracurricular, were most important to you as these are the topics on which you should focus in your statement. It is important to understand that your personal statement is just that; it is personal (see "Personal statement myths"). The best personal statements have excellent flow and tell a vivid and intriguing story about the applicant and those experiences that have shaped the applicant's path the most. Your personal statement should include what influenced your decisions and demonstrate thought, insight, and introspection. You do not want your personal statement to simply regurgitate your application entries.

The conclusion

In your conclusion, it is customary to "go full circle" by coming back to the topic—or anecdote—you introduced in the introduction, but this is not a must. Your conclusion should address what you hope to achieve and your goals for medical school.

Personal statement myths*

Myth #1: Never write about anything that took place in the past or before college. This myth is one of my favorites. Your goal is to give admissions committees a complete picture of who you are, what motivates you, and how your interests have evolved. For most of the clients with whom I work, these pivotal experiences occurred well before they made the decision to apply to medical school; this makes sense since it takes years to complete the prerequisites needed to apply. While you don't want to dwell on something that happened in the distant past, if one of your most motivating experiences was in high school or even grade school, then you should mention it.

The only caveat to this advice is that writing about events early in childhood is never convincing. It is unlikely, for example, that you really remember what happened to you when you were 4.

Myth #2: Never write about topics unrelated to medicine. If you are an accomplished musician, artist or athlete, you won't want to write an entire essay on this topic, but if some significant activity or event in the past influenced your path or relates to or parallels your interest in medicine, then, by all means, mention it in your personal statement. With their emphasis on the holistic review of applicants, admissions committees are seeking diverse applicants and the definition of diversity is broad. No one expects that you have spent your entire life in the library, a lab, or a doctor's office. That said, most of what you write about in your essay should in some way be linked to your motivation to pursue your desired career.

Myth #3: Never write about a patient encounter or your own experience with health care. I hear this from applicants all the time: "But, everyone writes about patients. I want to be different." "My roommate from last year wrote about her grandmother's death. That seems so cliché." Some topics are indeed common, but what is not uniform is how applicants write about them. Everyone has different stories, observations, and insights. So, while some topics may superficially seem similar or "popular," your perceptions and description of how these experiences influenced you need not be trite. I have read hundreds (actually, probably thousands) of essays about patient encounters and illness, yet the good ones still stand out and tell me so much about the applicant's motivation, character, maturity, and insight. Not only is what you choose to write about important, but how you convey your insightful thoughts and ideas on that topic is equally so.

Myth #4: Always have a theme or a thesis. Every year applicants tell me: "I showed the personal statement to my (premed advisor/uncle/sister/ mom's friend who is a doctor), and he said it is awful because I don't have a theme." Most personal statements don't have a theme or a thesis. What is important is that your essay has "flow" and good transitions. With about a one page limit, it is tough to develop a strong theme in an essay and this isn't really the goal of the personal statement. It should tell your story, and that story usually doesn't have a theme. This doesn't mean that you shouldn't have "common threads" in your statement. For example, you may have multiple meaningful experiences that are all related to global health or working with the underserved. I have read only a handful of personal statements that have had a well-defined theme or thesis.

Myth #5: Don't write about anything negative. You never want to bad-mouth anything or anyone in your essay, yet I find that this good advice has been extended to "never write about a negative or less-than-sunny experience." For example, if you had a poor undergraduate academic performance because a close family member got sick or because of transition issues and were terribly homesick and immature, you should address the negative experience and explain what happened and why. Or, maybe you had difficulty during your childhood because you were an immigrant or were underprivileged. I commonly hear, "I don't want to write about that. Yes, it was important but I don't want to tell a sob story or sound negative." As long as you write about your experiences in terms of how they helped you to grow and how they influenced your choices, admissions officers will not perceive you in a bad light.

* This box is based on an article I wrote for the Student Doctor Network.

CHAPTER 20

INSTITUTIONAL ACTION/ MISDEMEANOR/FELONY SECTIONS

First of all, be sure to check with your college registrar if you have incurred an institutional action. Some students unwittingly fill out this section for the wrong reasons, and you want to complete this section only if you must. I have found that some college premed advisors have also misguided students about what is considered an institutional action. This section is not used to explain bad grades. But if you had an institutional action it is important to explain, matter-of-factly, what happened, why it happened, and what you learned. Express remorse or regret for the incident, and explain clearly that you now see the errors you made. If you have taken any actions as a result of the incident, write about that as well.

Sometimes misdemeanors or felonies can be difficult to overcome depending on the severity of the incident. Medical school admissions committees can be unforgiving if you exhibited violence, impulsive behavior, dishonesty, or unprofessional behaviors. However, some incidents can be overlooked. If you show remorse and understanding in your writing and then on your interview, the admissions committee might see beyond your past poor judgment.

For example, if you incurred a driving under the influence misdemeanor, and you are now teaching high school students about what can happen if you drink and drive, include this information in the description. You have 1,325 characters (with spaces) to write this section.

CHAPTER 21

DISADVANTAGED STATUS

Disadvantaged status is self-determined and should be based on whether or not you grew up in an underserved area, or if your family received state or federal aid assistance. Admissions committees absolutely need to know if you came from an underserved background. Why? Growing up with few means yet successfully applying to medical school demonstrates perseverance, commitment, and the ability to overcome great adversity. Also, individuals from underserved areas will be more likely to return, as physicians, to care for underserved communities and will also act as much-needed role models for young people in these communities. Therefore, it is in our society's best interest that we make a medical education accessible for individuals who are from low income households. Many premedical programs designed for minority, underserved, and underrepresented individuals are available.

Not having the resources, role models, and financial luxuries that others had will distinguish you from other candidates and put you in a different category. Be honest in your description of your background. Where did you live? What were your resources? Did you work during high school and college? Will you be or were you the first in your family to graduate from college? You are allowed 1,325 characters (with spaces) to write this section.

CV/resume

Once you become a doctor, you will never refer to your "resume" again. From this point on, you will call your resume a "CV" (curriculum vitae). You do not need a CV for the medical school admissions process, but you will need one when you seek out summer opportunities, and some letter writers may routinely request a CV. I encourage all students and residents to always have an up to date resume available and to update it regularly.

PART 5

EXAMPLES OF EFFECTIVE DOCUMENTS: EXPERIENCE DESCRIPTIONS, MOST MEANINGFUL SUMMARIES, AND PERSONAL STATEMENT

In the following chapters, we introduce several medical school applicants and reproduce their application documents. These documents represent a composite picture of the applications of various successful candidates. These documents were composed by successful medical school applicants although the personal details and identifying information have been changed to protect the applicants' identities.

CHAPTER 22

MEET AMY:
AN APPLICANT TO MEDICAL SCHOOL

We will use Amy to illustrate the general process of writing an application to medical school, along with providing the resulting documents. Amy will first list those experiences, personal, extracurricular, and scholarly, that have been most influential in two areas: her life in general and her path to medical school. She will put this personal inventory in chronologic order for use in composing her personal statement. She will then select those experiences that were the most significant to her and will reflect and think about why they were important. For her application entries, Amy will write about each experience, including those that she considers influential in her life but not in her choice of medicine, in her application entries. Experiences that Amy will not write about in her activity entries or her personal statement are those that she does not consider most influential in either her life or in her choice of medicine.

Amy's personal inventory (from oldest to most recent)

1. Going with my mom to work. She is a surgeon

— I was very curious about what she did. I was intrigued by the relationships she had with patients and how much they valued her efforts. I also loved seeing her as "a doctor" since, to me, she was just "mom."

2. I loved biology in high school. I started to think seriously about medicine then. It was during high school that I became fascinated with biology and how the human body worked. I would say that was when I thought, "Hmm, maybe I should be a doctor."

3. Grandmother's death, senior year of high school. My grandmother's death was tragic. It was the first time I had ever seen someone close to me suffer. It was one of the most devastating experiences in my life.

4. Global Health Trip to Guatemala my freshman year of college. I realized after going to Guatemala that I had always taken my access to health care for granted. Here I saw children who didn't have basic health care. This made me want to become a physician so I could give more to people like those I met in Guatemala.

5. Sorority involvement. Even though sorority life might seem trivial, I loved it. I learned to work with different types of people and gained some really valuable leadership experience.

6. Poor grades in college science classes. I still regret that I did badly in my science classes. I think I was immature and was also too involved in other activities and didn't have the focus I needed to do well.

7. Teaching and tutoring Jose, a child from Honduras. In a way, meeting Jose in a college tutoring program brought my Guatemala experience to my home. Jose struggled academically, and his parents were immigrants and spoke only Spanish, so they had their own challenges. I tried to help Jose as much as I could. I saw that because he lacked resources, he was at a tremendous disadvantage.

8. Volunteering at Excellent Medical Center. Shadowing physicians at the medical center gave me a really broad view of medicine. I learned about different specialties, met many different patients, and saw both great and not-so-great physician role models.

9. Counselor at Ronald McDonald House. Working with sick kids made me appreciate my health. I tried to make them happy and was so impressed with their resilience. It made me realize that good health is everything.

10. Oncology research. Understanding what happens behind the scenes in research was fascinating. Not only did I gain some valuable research experience, but I learned how research is done.

11. Peer health counselor. Communicating with my peers about really important medical tests gave me an idea of the tremendous responsibility that doctors have. I also learned that it is important to be sensitive, to listen, and to be open-minded when working with others.

12. Clinical Summer Program. This gave me an entirely new view of medicine. I worked with the forensics department, and visiting scenes of deaths was entirely new to me. This experience

added a completely new dimension to my understanding of medicine and how illness and death affect loved ones.

13. Emergency department internship. Here I learned so much about how things worked in the hospital. I realized how important it was that people who worked in the clinical department were involved in creating hospital policies. This made me understand, in practical terms, how an MPH would give me the foundation to make even more change in the future.

14. Master's in public health. I decided to get an MPH for two reasons. First of all, I knew my undergraduate science GPA was an issue so I figured that graduate level courses in which I performed well would boost my record. I don't think I will write this on my application, but I also thought the degree would give me other skills if I didn't get into medical school, and I knew it would also give me something on which I could build during medical school and in my career since I was interested in policy work.

As you can see from Amy's personal inventory list, she has many accomplishments that are important to her and influenced her path. The most influential personal experience that motivated her to practice medicine was her mother's career as a practicing physician, but Amy was also motivated by watching her mother's career evolve. Even though the death of her grandmother was devastating for Amy, she did not consider this experience especially influential in her choice to attend medical school so she didn't write about it in her personal statement.

Amy wrote an experience-based personal statement, rich with anecdotes and detailed descriptions, to illustrate the evolution of her interest in medicine and how this motivated her to also earn a master's in public health.

Here is Amy's application, presented in the order it was likely to be read; first are her application entries, then her personal statement. Remember, under the new AMCAS® rules, each experience entry is limited to 700 characters, except for three "most meaningful" experiences, which get a separate discussion, using up to 1,325 characters, in addition to and immediately following the 700 character description. The first three experiences listed below from Amy's application—marked with an asterisk (*)—are her "most meaningful" choices. The actual application, however, will automatically list all experiences in chronologic order.

Amy's application:

EXPERIENCE

*Experience Type: Research/Lab
Experience Description: Summer Research Program
Contact Name: Mr. Smith
Organization Name: The Clinic
City / State /Country
Dates: 7/20XX – 8/20XX

Experience Description: The research program in which I participated gave me a very well rounded understanding of medicine. My responsibilities included working on a research project and presenting my findings at the conclusion of the program. Because of my interest in public health, I chose to work with Dr. Smith on a project focusing on HIV/AIDS. I also shadowed many physicians, assisting with simple tasks such as cleaning rooms or transporting patients.

Most Meaningful Experience Summary: While working at the clinic I met Joshua, a middle-aged, friendly man, who had suffered from uncontrolled diabetes for many years. Due to this illness, a digit on his right foot had been amputated, and he was slowly losing his vision. His eyes teared as he discussed his fear of not being able to see his 5-year old grandson play 'futbol.' I spoke with the physician about Joshua's condition and asked why his diabetes was poorly controlled. He explained that Joshua only recently qualified for Medicaid and was never able to afford private insurance, so he had not received the care he needed. This experience helped me understand how people suffer when they lack access to care.

By shadowing physicians and attending rounds and resident meetings for more than 50 hours per week, in nearly every medical specialty, I learned about the reality of a physician's life. I also led the development and implementation of a public health HIV/AIDS research project entitled "Testing Earlier and Mitigating AIDS" and presented my findings at the annual Research Symposium. The hospital system used the data to develop routine point of care HIV testing for the hospital system, affecting nearly 500,000 patients annually.

> *Experience Type: Research/Lab
> Experience Description: Oncology Research
> Contact Name: Dr. Smith
> Organization Name: Medical Center
> City / State /Country
> Dates: 12/20XX – 6/20XX

Experience Description: I worked in an oncology lab's cell culture core lab, where I assisted in development of new cell lines from tumor samples, which were then tested in mouse models. After establishing and characterizing cell lines and assuring their purity, we distributed them worldwide to be used by other labs for research. I participated in the genetic fingerprinting of cell lines by conducting multiple DNA and RNA PCR, learned many other laboratory procedures, and maintained the database of thousands of frozen samples.

Most Meaningful Experience Summary: My interest in learning more about medical research led me to Dr. Excellent Mentor. The focus of Dr. Mentor's laboratory, and the program that he leads, was to develop more effective treatments for certain types of cancers. This lab serves as the reference lab for a national and local cancer group for establishing new cell cultures and testing agents against cancer on these cultures. Members of the lab designed phase I and II trials for potential new drug treatments. I gained a thorough understanding of clinical trials and how long it takes to make progress. It helped me understand the importance of appreciating the clinical implications of work that is done and motivated my interest in research. On several occasions, I was able to shadow oncologists, which helped me understand how desperate patients and their families are to find cures. The compassion these doctors demonstrated is something I hope to emulate. Although I would have loved to continue working in this lab, Dr. Mentor relocated to New York to lead the new Cancer Center at Prestigious Medical School.

*Experience Type: Teaching/Tutoring
Experience Description: Education
Project for Underserved Children
Contact Name: Mr. Smith
Organization Name: Education Center
City / State /Country: Anytown, USA
Dates: 9/20XX – 5/20XX

Experience Description: As a tutor, I worked with many underserved children, helping them complete their homework and understand concepts. I tutored the same child over the course of the year for four hours per week. Not only did I learn about the academic challenges these children faced, but I also understood the hurdles they had to overcome outside the classroom. Many didn't speak English or spoke limited English and therefore their education helped their entire families.

Most Meaningful Experience Summary: Jose's family immigrated to the US from Honduras. His father was a custodian, and his mother stayed at home with his six siblings. When I first began working with Jose, he was reluctant to speak English since he spoke only Spanish at home. Jose had to simultaneously master oral and written English. We painstakingly completed his grammar exercises, read Dr. Seuss, and practiced writing his letters. Initially he was unable to scribble the six letters in his name, but only eight months later, he had become one of the best readers in his class.

Jose was a student in downtown Houston whom I tutored while participating in the Education Project, one of the oldest and largest service-learning projects in the country. I mentored groups of two to five students weekly; we reviewed academic concepts and discussed a variety of social issues they faced. This program immersed me in the community and gave me a greater understanding of the challenges immigrants face. I discovered that to help others learn and understand, I must be knowledgeable about their home environment and personal challenges. Further, patiently sitting with Jose as he sounded out words and congratulating him on his success made me realize the importance and satisfaction of motivating others to succeed.

> **Experience Type: Other**
> **Experience Description: Emergency Department Internship**
> **Contact Name: Mr. Smith**
> **Organization Name: Medical Center**
> **City / State /Country**
> **Dates: 2/20XX – present**

Experience Description: In the emergency department, I analyze and map patient flow for discharge patients. I have identified key inefficiencies that decrease patient throughput time for the emergency department. I track patients for eight hours per day through each point of contact for their entire visit, from their arrival at the ED through discharge. I presented my preliminary findings to administrators at an operations committee meeting and made practical recommendations to improve throughput. The entire process, on average, requires 10 hours, of which 35% is spent in the discharge process alone. The medical center has implemented many of my recommendations as standard protocol.

**Experience Type: Leadership
– not listed elsewhere
Experience Description: Undergraduate
and Graduate Leadership
Contact Name: Ms. Smith
Organization Name: Greek Organization
City / State /Country
Dates: 9/20XX – 6/20XX**

Experience Description: I held a variety of leadership roles as an undergraduate and graduate student. 1) I was elected by my peers to the Student Health Council Executive Board, Master in Health Administration's Student Advisory Committee, and serve as Events Chair. 2) I was elected by the Pan Hellenic Board from thousands of undergraduate Greek members to serve on the Pan Hellenic Council as a Recruitment Counselor. 3) As an undergraduate peer mediator, I resolved disputes between students in a formal and confidential setting. I was selected by the Executive Board as Director of Finance. 4) I was one of 20 people selected for Theresas out of the 200 students who applied for membership.

**Experience Type: Community Service/
Volunteer – not Medical/Clinical
Experience Description: Ronald McDonald House
Contact Name: Mr. Smith
Organization Name: Ronald McDonald House
City / State /Country
Dates: 7/20XX – 8/20XX**

Experience Description: As a counselor at this camp, which featured typical summer camp offerings, I gained an understanding of the devastating effects of chronic illness on children. As I supervised these children on horseback rides and in the pool, or helped them climb the 50 foot tower, I became aware of their strength and resilience. I was also inspired by the selfless group of individuals who ran the camp, eagerly putting their own lives on hold to provide campers with the carefree environment they craved and deserved. This experience helped confirm that I wanted a career as a pediatrician.

Experience Type: Community Service/ Volunteer – Medical/Clinical
Experience Description: Peer Health Counselor
Contact Name: Mr. Smith
Organization Name: Medical Center
City / State /Country
Dates: 12/20XX – 5/20XX

Experience Description: As a peer counselor in the Student Health Department, I was part of a select team of students chosen, following a written application, interview and 25 – hour training session, to educate the community on healthful prevention methods, manage the resource room, administer HIV testing, and counsel patients after receiving lab results. During my first year, HIV testing involved a two-week, pre – and post-week process, where the client came in for the swab the first week and received the results only after another week filled with anxiety. I helped institute rapid point-of-care HIV testing for the community, which eliminated the need for follow up.

Experience Type: Leadership
– not Listed Elsewhere
Experience Description: Greek Council
Contact Name: Mr. Smith
Organization Name: Greek Organization
City / State /Country
Dates: 8/20XX – 5/20XX

Experience Description: When I was a sophomore, my peers selected me, out of my house's other 125 members, to the position of house representative to the council, the Greek school-wide governing board, representing more than 800 women. In this position, I served as a liaison between my chapter and the council, attended weekly meetings with both the governing body and my chapter, and helped plan sponsored events for my sorority, to nurture relations between the thousands of women in the Greek system. I was again elected by my peers to the position of external social chair and networked with 25 Greek organizations to help organize the transportation, food, venue, and entertainment of social events for 200 individuals.

> **Experience Type: Community Service/ Volunteer – Medical/Clinical**
> **Experience Description: Operation Smile**
> **Contact Name: Mr. Smith**
> **Organization Name: Operation Smile**
> **City / State /Country**
> **Dates: 9/20XX – 5/20XX**

Experience Description: My involvement with Operation Smile, a non-profit that advocates for sustainable healthcare, was especially meaningful. I joined this organization as an incoming freshman. During my junior year, I served as director of events, organizing a widespread marketing campaign to promote both the organization and our events to our school and local community. The following year, as VP, I worked with the president to organize fundraising and community events.

While I was on the executive board, our chapter donated more money than any other chapter to the national organization. I was elected president and have since focused on increasing awareness of the organization.

Experience Type: Teaching/Tutoring
Experience Description: Academic Tutoring
Contact Name: Mr. Smith
Organization Name: Tutoring Center
City / State /Country
Dates: 8/20XX – 1/20XX

Experience Description: As a tutor, I mentored academically at-risk athletes, assisting them in their studies of Spanish, biology, English, philosophy, and psychology. I worked with them individually to increase their understanding of academic concepts and to motivate them to learn. JP was enrolled in a philosophy course to fulfill a general education level requirement. He routinely arrived at our weekly sessions without his materials, despite my encouragement and reminders. Every session we spent together, I reiterated my confidence in his abilities and identified specific improvements he had made since the previous week. JP earned a final grade of C+; this was the highest grade on his transcript.

Experience Type: Community Service/
Volunteer – Medical/Clinical
Experience Description: Global Medical Brigade
Contact Name: Mr. Smith
Organization Name: Guatemala
City / State /Country
Dates: 5/20XX – 5/20XX

Experience Description: I helped organize our first Global Medical Brigade to Guatemala. For five months, the co-founders and I solicited medical organizations to provide supplies, medications, and volunteers. We partnered with a local Guatemalan philanthropy to construct five makeshift medical clinics. We offered care and distributed medicines in rural parts of Guatemala to more than 1,000 residents who have no access to medical care, or the financial capacity to purchase simple preventive self-care tools, such as toothbrushes. This humbling experience elucidated how much we take for granted in the United States. I learned about the challenges faced by individuals who don't have access to medical care.

Experience Type: Honors/Awards/Recognitions
Experience Description: Award Recipient
Contact Name: Mr. Smith
Organization Name: College
City / State /Country
Dates: 5/20XX

Experience Description: As an undergraduate student, I have been recognized for my academic achievements by earning a place on the Dean's List nearly every semester. The Dean's List recognizes students who have achieved a GPA of 3.5 or higher.

I have been accepted to various academic honor societies based on GPA and my volunteer and work experience, including Biological Sciences Honors Society, Pre-medical Honors Society, Delta Delta Delta, Alpha Alpha, the College Honor's Society, Gamma Gamma where I served as the VP of relations, Phi Phi Sophomore Scholars, The Order of Omega, Rho Lambda, and the Blue and Golden Key National Honor Societies, among others.

Experience Type: Community Service/
Volunteer – Medical/Clinical
Experience Description: Clinical Volunteer
Contact Name: Mr. Smith
Organization Name: Medical Center
City / State /Country
Dates: 3/20XX – 9/20XX

Experience Description: I worked with doctors, residents, and medical students in the departments of ob/gyn and emergency medicine at Excellent Medical Center. I watched as physicians and nurses delivered premature infants, stabilized gunshot victims, and cared for a diverse patient population. I also learned that many patients in the US lack access to medical care. I talked with the patients, helped in the triage process, or served as an assistant for procedures. I comforted patients with my words and gained a broad understanding of how medicine is practiced. These experiences motivated my interest in health care policy.I recently volunteered for the Medical Volunteer Corps during a week long clinic in Houston.

**Experience
Type: Extracurricular/Hobbies/Avocations
Experience Description: Travel/Hobbies
Contact Name:
Organization Name:
City / State /Country
Dates:**

Experience Description: My passion for travel has led me to study abroad in London as an undergraduate student and to visit various countries and continents around the globe, including South America, Japan, and Israel. Such experiences have afforded me the opportunity to understand how different cultures and individuals live and interact.

Although biking and cooking are other activities I truly enjoy, I have found that the people I meet and bond with while pursuing my interests are the true driving force behind many of my chosen free-time experiences. Being able to interact with diverse groups of people is another significant benefit to practicing medicine, which I will take advantage of throughout my career.

PERSONAL COMMENTS
(Even though most people call this section the "personal statement," AMCAS® terms it "personal comments.")

She was sprawled across the floor of her apartment. Scattered trash, decaying food, alcohol bottles, medication vials, and cigarette butts covered the floor. I had just graduated from college, and this was my first day on rotation with the forensic pathology department as a Summer Scholar, one of my most valuable activities on the path to medical school. As the coroner deputy scanned the scene for clues to what caused this woman's death, I saw her distraught husband. I did not know what to say other than "I am so sorry." I listened intently as he repeated the same stories about his wife and his dismay that he never got to say goodbye. The next day, alongside the coroner as he performed the autopsy, I could not stop thinking about the grieving man.

Discerning a cause of death was not something I had previously associated with the practice of medicine. As a child, I often spent Saturday mornings with my mother, a surgeon, as she rounded on patients. I witnessed the results of her actions, as she provided her patients a renewed chance at life. I grew to honor and respect my mother's profession. Witnessing the immense gratitude of her patients and their families, I quickly came to admire the impact she was able to make in the lives of her patients and their loved ones.

I knew I wanted to pursue a career in medicine as my mother had, and throughout high school and college I sought out clinical, research, and volunteer opportunities to gain a deeper understanding of medicine. After volunteering with cancer survivors at Camp Ronald McDonald, I was inspired to further understand this disease. Through my oncology research, I learned about therapeutic processes for treatment development. Further, following my experience administering HIV tests, I completed research on point-of-care HIV testing, to be instituted throughout 26 hospitals and clinics. I realized that research often served as a basis for change in policy and medical practice and sought out opportunities to learn more about both.

All of my medically related experiences demonstrated that people who were 'behind the scenes' and had limited or no clinical background made many of the decisions in health care. Witnessing the evolution of my mother's career further underscored the impact of policy change on the practice of medicine. In particular, the limits legislation imposed on the care she could provide influenced my perspective and future goals. Patients whom my mother had successfully treated for more than a decade, and with whom she had long-standing, trusting relationships, were no longer able to see her, because of policy coverage changes. Some patients, frustrated by these limitations, simply stopped seeking the care they needed. As a senior in college, I wanted to understand how policy transformations came about and gain the tools I would need to help effect administrative and policy changes in the future as a physician. It was with this goal in mind that I decided to complete a master's in public health program before applying to medical school.

As an MPH candidate, I am gaining insight into the theories and practices behind the complex interconnections of the health care system; I am learning about economics, operations, management, ethics, policy, finance, and technology and how these entities converge to impact delivery of care. A holistic understanding of this diverse, highly competitive, market-driven system will allow me, as a clinician, to find solutions to policy, public health, and administration issues. I believe that change can be more effective if those who actually practice medicine also decide where improvements need to be made.

For example, as the sole intern for the emergency department at County Medical Center, I worked to increase efficiency in the ED by evaluating and mapping patient flow. I tracked patients from point of entry to point of discharge and found that the discharge process took up nearly 35% of patients' time. By analyzing the reasons for this situation, in collaboration with nurses and physicians who worked in the ED and had an intimate understanding of what took place in the clinical area, I was able to make practical recommendations to decrease throughput time. The medical center has already implemented these suggestions, resulting in decreased length of stays. This example illustrates the benefit of having clinicians who work 'behind the scenes' establish policies and procedures, impacting operational change and improving patient care. I will also apply what I have learned through this project as the business development intern at Another Local Medical Center this summer, where I will assist in strategic planning, financial analysis, and program reviews for various clinical departments.

Through my mother's career and my own medical experiences, I have become aware of the need for clinician administrators and policymakers. My primary goal as a physician will be to care for patients, but with the knowledge and experience I have gained through my MPH, I also hope to effect positive public policy and administrative changes.

Amy's personal statement structure

Paragraphs 1 and 2: Amy started her personal statement by illustrating a powerful experience she had when she realized that medical caregivers often feel impotent, and how this contrasted with her understanding of medicine as a little girl going with her mother to work. Recognition of this intense contrast also highlights Amy's maturity.

Paragraph 3: Amy then "lists" a few experiences that were important to her.

Paragraph 4: Amy describes the commonality in some of her experiences and how her observations were substantiated by watching the evolution of her mother's practice. She then explains how this motivated her to earn an MPH so she could create change more effectively as a physician than as a layman.

Paragraph 5: Amy then explains how her graduate degree is helping her to better understand the "issues in medicine" that she observed.

Paragraph 6: Amy then describes one exceptional accomplishment she had that highlights what she has learned and how she has applied it.

Paragraph 7: Finally, Amy effectively concludes her personal statement and summarizes the major topics addressed in her essay.

As you can see, Amy's statement has excellent flow, is captivating and unusual, and illustrates her understanding of, and commitment to, medicine. She also exhibits, throughout her application entries and statement, the personal competencies, characteristics, and qualities that medical school admissions officers are seeking. Her application also has broad appeal; reviewers who are focused on research, cultural awareness, working with the underserved, health administration and policy, teaching, or clinical medicine would all find it of interest. She also makes her application entries comprehensive enough that a reader might be satisfied by them alone and choose not to read her personal statement before checking off the "invite for interview" box on the screener's evaluation sheet. Amy does not write about every experience she has had in her personal statement, and she chooses her three "most meaningful" entries to explain those experiences that have been the most influential on her path to medicine. Even though her emergency department experience was especially valuable, she did not choose this as a "most meaningful" experience since she wrote about it, in depth, in her personal statement. And, even with only 700 characters for her standard experience entries, she was still able to demonstrate reflection and insight. Her application entries and personal statement complement each other very well, and are not unnecessarily repetitious, and her application as a whole is enjoyable to read.

Like many applicants, Amy's background was not flawless so it was important that her written application materials stand out from her competitors and that the flaws in her application be minimized. With MCATs® of 22 on her first attempt, a 30 on her second attempt, and an overall undergraduate science GPA of 3.3, Amy was not a shoe-in to medical school. Amy nonetheless earned acceptances to several excellent medical schools that most observers consider "middle tier" United States allopathic medical schools. Her compelling documents required a tremendous amount of introspection, time, and many, many revisions to produce final drafts. Remember, even if your academic background isn't perfect, you can get accepted to medical school!

CHAPTER 23

MEET MAGGIE:
EXPERIENCE DESCRIPTIONS, MOST MEANINGFUL SUMMARIES, AND PERSONAL STATEMENT

Maggie was an outstanding applicant with exceptional research and community service experiences. She attended a prestigious undergraduate institution yet earned an 8 in one of the science sections of the MCAT® and had a composite score of 29. Her GPA also was below 3.5 early in her college career. Composing documents that distinguished her from candidates with higher scores and grades therefore was a key component to her success. Maggie now attends an excellent medical school in the Northeast.

EXPERIENCE

*Experience Type: Research/Lab
Experience Name: Research
Contact Name & Title:
Organization Name: City / State / Country:
Experience Description:
Dates: 9/20XX – present

Experience Description: My role in the research lab is to study new vaccines and their protective functions. I perform basic laboratory procedures, including PCR and DNA sequencing, and I also manage our mouse colony. I often work independently to develop our experiments but also present my findings and progress at weekly research meetings. This is a full-time job, which has helped me understand the tremendous amount of time required to perform valuable research.

Most Meaningful Experience Summary: The great protection that vaccines offer against debilitating diseases motivates my research at the infectious disease department of The Medical Center. My work focuses on investigating candidate vaccines and adjuvant formulations that provide enhanced protective responses against a variety of infectious diseases at the preclinical level. Working with mice to investigate highly pathogenic diseases has allowed me to develop critical thinking skills and provide leadership to others while conducting experiments in a high-risk environment.

Analysis of the data and development of new experiments have driven my dedication. Comparing different formulations, immunization techniques, and antigen responses in various animal models gives me the opportunity to apply science to improving clinical outcomes. The goal of moving research forward for human benefits drives my work as I investigate the immunogenic potential of new formulations and discover how micrograms of an adjuvant can completely change the biologic response to a given vaccination. These experiences provide a behind-the-scenes understanding of medicine and add to my desire to deliver care as a physician.

*Experience Type: Community Service/
Volunteer – Medical/Clinical
Experience Name: Adult Day Health Volunteer
Contact Name & Title:
Organization Name: City / State / Country:
Experience Description:
Dates: 8/20XX – present

Experience Description: The Adult Day Health Center is a comprehensive facility that offers a variety of services to members of the community. My duties at the Adult Day Health Center are to make sure patients are comfortable, address their basic needs such as thirst or hunger, or to simply offer them company. The Center serves a largely underserved and homeless population so I also help clients find places to stay, sift through our donated clothes pile to help them find clean garments, and seek out transportation for them.

Most Meaningful Experience Summary: I look forward to the Sunday mornings I spend with HIV patients. My conversations with them have revealed these patients' great physical suffering; I have also learned how HIV steals independence and inflicts solitude. These patient interactions illustrate the human toll of disease and enhances my dedication to serving others as a physician.

I make the most of the time I spend with these patients because I know that these interactions have great potential to make a difference. I reach out to the individuals who always sit alone, making sure they remember to order lunch. I enjoy making the child of a patient feel comfortable as his mom receives her medication. I encourage the patient working with his speech pathologist to use his alphabet card to better enunciate words while he discusses his favorite pop star with me over lunch.

Having come to learn and use the names of the Sunday crowd, I know I offer them an enhanced sense of security and belonging. Witnessing how diseases can affect mothers with small children and people of all races, ages and backgrounds and seeing the changes in the health of the patients I serve week to week have made me aware of the bleak realities of illness. This experience has increased my respect for individuals in need as well as my desire to serve them.

*Experience Type: Community Service/ Volunteer – Medical/Clinical
Experience Name: Hospice Volunteer
Contact Name & Title:
Organization Name: City / State / Country:
Experience Description:
Dates: 8/20XX – present

Experience Description: The hospice center serves patients who have incurable conditions and their families. They provide medical, emotional, and psychiatric support. My goals as a hospice volunteer are to visit with patients and their families, retrieve items they may need such as blankets, food, or water, and to assist staff with routine tasks. I also started our university student volunteer hospice program and spearhead fund raising efforts for our group.

Most Meaningful Experience Summary: As a volunteer at the hospice, I visit patients in their homes and at the hospital. My visits provide companionship, allow family members time to run essential errands, and offer an outlet to express concerns and emotions. By witnessing how the incredible stress serious illness places on patients and families makes even the minor tasks of daily living, such as filling out paperwork, overwhelming, I became aware of the blunt realities of disease. I treat all of my patients equally, offering the same respect to patients who cannot understand English, patients who refused service, and patients who just want someone to keep them company as they watch TV. These interactions allow me to appreciate the advocacy each patient requires, especially those with language barriers. Furthermore, the strength of patients as they fight to retain their dignity in light of debilitating conditions further motivates me to serve those in need.

Committed to hospice work, I served as the VP of a student run organization to raise money for the hospice by selling donated winter hats. The days spent selling hats in the freezing cold allowed us to increase awareness of hospice work and recruit many new volunteers.

> **Experience Type: Community Service/
> Volunteer – non – Medical/Clinical
> Experience Name: Mission Home
> Contact Name & Title:
> Organization Name: City / State / Country:
> Experience Description:
> Dates: 6/20XX – present**

Experience Description: Each Saturday morning I spend at the cafe with a filled coffee thermos in one hand and a bag of cups in another, I reach out to needy strangers on the street to tell them about the healthy and affordable meals available to everyone.

The cafe offers a dignified atmosphere for the city's homeless and transient population. For many, it is the first step towards a self-sustaining lifestyle as patrons must pay or work in the kitchen to earn their meals. Wanting a safe and comfortable place to eat may seem basic, but for some it is a luxury. I work with homeless individuals to serve meals and clean dishes and have come to appreciate the variety of experiences and perspectives they offer.

Experience Type: Research/Lab
Experience Name: Research
Contact Name & Title:
Organization Name: City / State / Country:
Experience Description:
Dates: 1/20XX – 6/20XX

Experience Description: My work inspired me to join the lab to investigate an advanced immunotherapy technique. I examined the use of an engineered cell line to serve as antigen presenting cells to activate and expand tumor reactive human CD8+ T cells that can augment the immune response to cancer. My work focused on conducting the preliminary studies necessary to create a master cell bank from which these engineered cells could be further investigated in clinical trials. I presented my research at the Student Research Symposium. The good manufacturing practices facility in which I conducted my research gave me the opportunity to work at the point where research transitions from the bench to the clinic.

Experience Type: Research/Lab
Experience Name: Research
Contact Name & Title:
Organization Name: City / State / Country:
Experience Description:
Dates: 5/20XX – 9/20XX

Experience Description: The drug development process was obscure to me, and I intended to learn firsthand how an idea could be developed into a clinically relevant therapy. The lab was developing technology to activate and expand patient T-cells ex-vivo and then to reintroduce the immune cells back into the patient's body to help fight off a range of diseases from cancers to HIV. The broad clinical application of this novel idea quickly increased my interest in the potential of treatments and motivated my future interest in medical research. I quickly learned how research allows for the translation of textbook science into valuable clinical tools.

Experience Type: Other
Experience Name: Residential Assistant
Contact Name & Title:
Organization Name: City / State / Country:
Experience Description:
Dates: 9/20XX – 5/20XX

Experience Description: It was a great privilege to live in the Infectious Disease Residential Program during my freshman year at college. By learning about different diseases on a daily basis, and living in an environment in which scientific discussions were ubiquitous, this program increased my interest in medicine. Hall events included conversational discussions of diseases among residents, movie nights focusing on disease thrillers, and faculty talks.

The inquisitive thinking and sharing of ideas among physicians allowed me to appreciate the communication necessary for efficient diagnosis and control of diseases. Equally important, the compassion displayed by the physicians was admirable.

Experience Type: Research/Lab
Experience Name: Research
Contact Name & Title:
Organization Name: City / State / Country:
Experience Description:
Dates: 9/20XX – 1/20XX

Experience Description: I witnessed how depression could eat away at one's self-worth and sense of purpose and became fascinated by how an outwardly invisible psychological problem can plague a physically healthy individual. I worked at the Depression Study where I discussed the details of our clinical trials with patients. I explained our investigation of the use of psychotherapy alone or in conjunction with medication therapy and the need for a placebo group. Hearing the desperate willingness of these patients to join our studies emphasized the debilitating nature of this mental illness.

I assisted in conducting cross-meta analyses of different treatment options for adolescent depression.

Experience Type: Community Service/
Volunteer – non – Medical/Clinical
Experience: Neuroscience Fair
Contact Name & Title:
Organization Name: City / State / Country:
Experience Description:
Dates: 5/20XX – present

Experience Description: I spearheaded efforts to create projects for the Kids Judge Neuroscience Fair. This fair allows students to judge neuroscience projects developed by undergraduates. We gave the students a chance to learn how the brain is involved in processing information by conducting interactive mini-experiments on the senses.

Among our many experiments was one where I asked the kids to taste jellybeans while pinching their noses to demonstrate the interactions between olfaction and gustatory neurons. Explaining how the brain processes both taste and smell enabled the kids to understand why they could not enjoy their dinner when they were sick. Our project was awarded first prize.

Experience Type: Research/Lab
Experience Name: Research
Contact Name & Title:
Organization Name: City / State / Country:
Experience Description:
Dates: 9/20XX – 1/20XX

Experience Description: I immersed myself in the workings of the brain and its dysfunctions to gain a more complete understanding of these disorders. My project at the neurobiology lab at the university investigated the connections between brain regions of mice that are linked to anxiety disorders.

The biologic awareness I developed while working with mice, injecting minuscule amounts of dye into their brains and perfusing their tissues to prepare slides for staining, increased my appreciation of biology and the biologic basis of mental disorders. Furthermore, the sensitive nature of this work highlighted the need for meticulous work and how directly the environment influences biology.

Experience Type: Community Service/
Volunteer – non – Medical/Clinical
Experience: Admissions Interviewer
Contact Name & Title:
Organization Name: City / State / Country:

Experience Description:
Dates: 5/20XX – 9/20XX

Experience Description: As the co-chair of The University's Secondary School Committee, I organized and conducted interviews with high school students, serving as an advocate for state students applying for admission to the university. This voluntary position allowed me to help dedicated students receive the education they crave.

For the application cycle, the admission interviewing system evolved from a paper to an online-based system. The logistical challenges of this change could have jeopardized the interview process, but by ensuring that all students applying from the state were given a chance to have an interview, our committee was one of the most successful in the country.

Experience Type: Teaching/Tutoring
Experience Name: Research
Contact Name & Title:
Organization Name: City / State / Country:
Experience Description:
Dates: 6/20XX – 1/20XX

Experience Description: I served as a volunteer for Community Tutoring where I introduced neuroscience to local high school and elementary students by developing and teaching interactive lessons. My classes ranged from a lesson on brain anatomy in which students used ordinary items to create a representation of the neuron to discussions of how biochemical warfare agents affect brain chemistry. I presented a lesson on psychiatric disorders and their biologic basis to the high school students to foster discussion about this often-taboo subject within the classroom.

My efforts to motivate my peers and youth about science's potential continues today as I am a mentor for the State Biotech Expo.

Experience Type: Awards/Honors
Experience Name: Honor Society
Contact Name & Title:
Organization Name: City / State / Country:
Experience Description:
Dates: 5/20XX

Experience Description: Honor Society brought together a diverse group of senior class students who had established themselves as leaders on campus. The synergy from our dedicated members allowed us to raise funds for the Coalition Against Hunger by hosting a successful Oktoberfest celebration. I worked to increase publicity for the event by spreading awareness throughout the community. We partnered with Goodwill and hosted the first "move-out clothing drive," which the Honor Society continues to host annually.

As the chair of the design committee, I worked to develop our logo and to design sweatshirts, allowing us to raise awareness of our work on campus.

Experience Type: Research/Lab
Experience Name: Research
Contact Name & Title:
Organization Name: City / State / Country:
Experience Description:
Dates: 6/20XX - 9/20XX

Experience Description: I witnessed the insidious nature of psychiatric disorders through my work in a clinical trial setting focused on investigating psychiatric medications. I participated in initial patient screenings where I listened to patients with a wide variety of mental illnesses describe their distinct symptoms of depression, bipolar disorder, or anxiety disorder. My experiences with patients highlighted the devastating nature of mental illness and compelled the compassion and attentiveness I offered while answering their questions about participating in clinical trials. In addition, I compiled data to find correlations between depression, body weight, and other factors.

*Examples of most meaningful experiences.

PERSONAL COMMENTS

Whether she was learning English with me or spending the summer helping me tend our cucumber patch, my grandmother supported my efforts to become the first generation of my family to attend college. Tragically, before my freshman year of high school, my grandmother's gastric cancer metastasized. The disease spread throughout her system and found its way into my life, challenging my entire way of living. Indeed, the ease and speed with which this invisible force removed the bedrock of my childhood exposed the brutal truth that we are biologic systems vulnerable to myriad threats.

At the same time, by witnessing my grandmother's strength as she inched her way out of bed to prepare herself for treatments, I became increasingly aware of the burning optimism that drives people to extend themselves through uncertainty. This direct exposure to the resilience of the human spirit as it battles disease initiated my desire to serve the infirm. Driven to research clinically relevant therapies and share my time and compassion with patients, my experiences have continuously fortified my desire to contribute to the field of medicine.

While still learning the basics of high school biology, a simple interaction with a friend's father serendipitously gave me a new understanding of the role of science in medicine that inspired me to action. As we talked in his office, he explained his research into a technology for treating a range of diseases. A glimpse at the broad therapeutic potential of this technology proved how science could produce tremendous clinical hope and piqued my interest in research. After completing my freshman year of college, I joined his research team as a summer intern to develop cost-effective mediums to help this investigational therapy become a reality for patients. While meticulously culturing cells in different mediums, graphing their growth and assaying their stability, I understood that my work was not singular and discrete, but that I was contributing to the hope of cancer and infectious disease patients. Realizing that the outskirts of knowledge contain such possibilities for great benefit further motivated me to explore the clinical potential of science. Moreover, my investigations led to awesome observations of swelling lymph nodes, enlarged spleens, and increased production of antibodies and cytokines, all of which affirm a blunt purpose – survival. Ultimately, the brilliance of our biologic reactions inspires my belief that by harnessing the responses that reflect our inherent will to survive, the potential therapies we can offer are unlimited.

Still, my admiration for the human spirit as it battles disease tremendously outweighs my amazement at the biologic responses the body launches to maintain health. Bridging all divides, health is our common foundation. Through my work with low-income HIV patients, I have learned about the loss of jobs, estrangement from family, and the solitude inflicted by HIV. The overreaching nature of HIV illustrates the devastating human toll of diseases. Yet merely by remembering patients' names and providing a listening ear as I serve meals, I provide these patients with a sense of belonging and support. Week to week, whether waking them up from their naps in time for lunch, or helping them find job training programs, I realize the great benefits of even such small acts of compassion, which increases my desire to offer these individuals much more. Equally important, by witnessing the struggles these patients face, even with the latest medications, I am reminded of the need to expand our biologic knowledge to produce better results.

Whether witnessing the symptoms of depression relapse after relapse, the infections caused by HIV that destroy an individual's ability to speak, or the weakness that follows chemotherapy, I am struck by the severity and diversity of biologic threats. Ultimately, the unlimited levels of trust, analysis, and compassion required to serve others in need drives my dedication and performance. Every aspect of my experiences – participating in research into the unknown, witnessing biologic responses that allow for a new day, and knowing patients like my grandmother who courageously continue through therapy – inspires me to contribute to the growing optimism medicine provides.

CHAPTER 24

MEET ADAM: DISADVANTAGED/CHILDHOOD INFORMATION, EXPERIENCE DESCRIPTIONS, MOST MEANINGFUL SUMMARIES, AND PERSONAL STATEMENT

Adam, an applicant who grew up with modest means, should be an inspiration to us all. Rather than allowing limited resources to stand in his way, Adam took advantage of everything that was available to him. Adam commuted to college from home and had a part-time job so he was stretched thin, and his initial college performance suffered. However, he worked hard and his grades improved. Most medical school admissions committees seek out applicants like Adam because, by overcoming adversity and succeeding with limited resources, they demonstrate exceptional perseverance, maturity, and dedication. Adam's accomplishments are, by themselves, impressive and he does an outstanding job of detailing his path, challenges, and commitment to medicine. Adam received multiple acceptances to top medical schools and was offered scholarships.

DISADVANTAGED/CHILDHOOD INFORMATION

Disadvantaged?: Yes

Explanation: I grew up in an inner city where few resources for healthcare and education were available. Our neighborhood was populated by minority groups who lacked the information necessary to obtain a private physician. When someone in my family was sick or needed vaccinations for school, we often made use of overcrowded free health clinics. My brothers went to local schools, sometimes attending classes in large trailers in which several classes took place simultaneously, but I was fortunate to attend magnet schools. While I did well in advanced placement courses in high school, I initially lacked the discipline and maturity necessary to excel in a university setting. Since my family knew nothing about higher education, I sought out advice and opportunities on my own. I also worked throughout high school and college, using my wages to contribute to my family and support my tuition. I lived at home during college to further assist my family by, for example, tutoring my brothers, taking them to school, and preparing meals when my parents worked late. Despite these challenges, I learned to balance work, family, and school and graduated cum laude.

EXPERIENCES

*Experience Type: Research/Lab
Experience Name: Research Study Assistant
Dates: 08/20XX – Until Present
Contact Name & Title: Clinical
Research Coordinator
Organization Name: Medical Center
City / State / Country: United States of America

Experience Description: I provide the Institutional Review Board (IRB) with the documentation necessary to conduct studies, assist with study start-up, identify eligible patients, obtain consent from patients, distribute study treatment, collect data, maintain data files, communicate with the IRB and study sponsors and train other research study assistants, and mentor employees interested in pre-health programs.

Most Meaningful Experience Summary: I manage studies examining the role of a drug in the prevention of erectile dysfunction following radical prostatectomy and the effect of pre-operative supplementation in prostate cancer patients. I also comanage studies seeking to develop new biomarkers in the detection of prostate cancer and assess differences in quality of life outcomes among patients who elect chemotherapy, radiotherapy, surgery, or active surveillance. Working in clinical research has provided me with the opportunity to directly apply my background in the sciences to improve patient care. I discovered an interest in explaining studies to patients who had little to no familiarity with urologic oncology. I also enjoyed mentoring newly hired staff who often had non-scientific backgrounds. The combination of teaching and applying my knowledge of science in a clinical setting has motivated my interest in academic medicine.

> ***Experience Type: Research/Lab**
> **Experience Name: Senior Project**
> **Dates: 01/20XX – 05/20XX**
> **Contact Name & Title: Professor**
> **Organization Name: University**
> **City / State / Country: United States of America**

Experience Description: My senior research project for my neuroscience major was titled, "Neuroprotective Effects of Conditioning in a Hemi-Parkinsonian Rat Model." With the guidance of my professor, I completed this project independently. I handled small animals, administered drugs, performed stereotaxic surgery, conducted behavioral exams, and examined neurotransmitter content via HPLC. I also did background research and wrote in detail about our findings and conclusions in my project paper.

Most Meaningful Experience Summary: The study examined the effect of an antioxidant in preventing the onset of Parkinson's disease (PD) in rats. A neurotoxin specific to dopaminergic neurons was injected into the substantia nigra of rats to induce the same damage caused by PD. This damage was assessed biochemically by measuring dopamine levels and behaviorally by examining motor function after stimulating dopaminergic receptors. Although the results were not statistically significant, rats conditioned with the neurotoxin generally had higher dopamine levels and greater motor control than rats that did not receive conditioning. Because motor functions in rats utilize the same neurologic pathway as do those functions in humans, results of the study could potentially lead to development of preventive supplements for patients at risk for PD. Through this experience, I improved my ability to think critically and analytically. I also gained a greater understanding of how research can influence patient care, and this motivated me to gain more clinical research experience after college.

    *Experience Type: Paid
    Employment – not Military
    Contact Name & Title: Pharmacist
    Organization Name: Pharmacy
    City / State / Country: United States of America

Experience Description: As a pharmacy technician, I prepared prescriptions for dispensing, billed medications to insurance, performed final billing transactions, ensured HIPAA compliance, and trained technicians. I communicated with patients, physicians, and staff and learned about basic pharmacology both on the job and through reading I did on my own.

Most Meaningful Experience Summary: This was my first experience interacting with patients. I quickly learned the importance of communication in healthcare, not solely between patients and pharmacists, but also between pharmacists and physicians. We went to great lengths to verify that patients received the correct medication and dosing instructions. I witnessed the importance of accountability in healthcare as each member of the pharmacy team who processed a prescription had to verify his or her work electronically via a fingerprint scanner. I observed the variations in accessibility to medication. The uninsured were almost always unable to afford antibiotics routinely paid for by insurance. Medicaid placed greater restrictions on medication formularies than private insurance groups did. At Pharmacy I learned that established treatments for given conditions were not always available for a particular patient because of limited supply or financial resources or lack of coverage. This helped me understand challenges facing patients as they try to "follow doctor's orders." One of my goals as a physician is to improve access to care and treatment for individuals who are underinsured.

Experience Type: Community Service/ Volunteer – not Medical/Clinical
Experience Name: Recruitment Team
Dates: 10/20XX – Until Present
Contact Name & Title:

Organization Name: University
City / State / Country: United States of America

Experience Description: I represent University at college fairs, participate in career networking events for current students, and conduct interviews for prospective students. In addition to assessing students' candidacy for admission, I share my experience as a student in each interview. My most memorable interview was with a prospective pre-health student whose parents immigrated to the US. The student excelled academically but lacked guidance. Having been in a similar situation, I provided the student with advice about coursework and internships. I enjoy the opportunity to give back to my college while providing students with the advice necessary to succeed and will continue to participate in this activity.

Experience Type:
Extracurricular/Hobbies/Avocations
Experience Name: Extracurricular Activities
Board Dates: 09/20XX – 05/20XX
Contact Name & Title: Mr. Advisor
Organization Name: University
City / State / Country: United States of America

Experience Description: I served as the Academic Category Representative. I was nominated by members of the University Student Activities Office because of my work in the Pre-Medical Society. I represented all academic organizations in weekly meetings where I helped determine whether newly formed student groups should receive university recognition. I also helped decide whether student events should receive university funds and approved/rejected budget proposals for all student-run organizations. I enjoyed my role because it allowed me to share my experiences in forming and maintaining the Pre-Medical Society while reaching out to the entire student body.

Experience Type: Research/Lab
Experience Name: Summer
Undergraduate Research Program
Dates: 05/20XX – 08/20XX
Contact Name & Title: Excellent Doctor
Organization Name: Excellent Medical School
City / State / Country: United States of America

Experience Description: I evaluated the efficacy of the D-dimer assay in predicting pulmonary emboli via comparisons of the assay with CT angiograms. I reviewed patient medical records, presented data weekly through written reports and PowerPoint presentations, and attended seminars on healthcare disparities and research development. Under the mentorship of Dr. Excellent, my project showed that while a positive D-dimer assay predicts abnormal clotting with more than 97% accuracy, it correlates with a pulmonary embolus only roughly half of the time. For the first time, the results of my study directly impacted doctors' clinical practice, and I took great pride in my work.

Experience Type: Presentations/Posters
Experience Name: Conference
Dates: 04/20XX Hours/Week:
Contact Name & Title: Professor
Organization Name:
City / State / Country: United States of America

Experience Description: I presented my study, entitled Awesome Study, which was conducted in The Laboratory, at The Conference. Although most of the students who attended majored in neurobiology, a few were from the field of psychobiology. Questions from the latter group allowed me to think about my project from a psychological perspective, and I used their input to enhance the study's design for my senior independent project. Their major concern was the control of stress-inducing factors that could skew my results.

Experience Type: Community Service/ Volunteer – not Medical/Clinical
Experience Name: Church Dates: 09/20XX – 06/20XX
Contact Name & Title: Director, Religious Education
Organization Name: St. Church
City / State / Country: United States of America

Experience Description: I taught Sunday school to third grade students. The curriculum was based on the Ten Commandments and helped create a moral foundation for decision making. I enjoyed teaching the class because the course focused on the development of morals though it was based on religion. The students came from diverse backgrounds and home environments and had different ways of determining the morality of their decisions. While students' preconceived notions of right and wrong were challenging at first, I learned to incorporate these differences in the curriculum.

Experience Type: Extracurricular/Hobbies/Avocations
Experience Name: President, Pre-Medical Society Dates: 08/20XX – 05/20XX
Contact Name & Title: Advisor
Organization Name: Pre-Medical Society
City / State / Country: United States of America

Experience Description: I planned events for students interested in careers related to healthcare. I invited alumni speakers, planned trips to medical school open houses, organized practice MCAT® sessions, and worked with other organizations for campus-wide events about health-related issues. I maintained the website. I collaborated with other organizations to hold service events, such as a campus-wide blood drive that annually attracts more than 200 donors. Events were also designed to increase campus awareness of HIV during AIDS week. Through an outside contractor, Pre-Med Society was able to provide anonymous oral HIV testing. We had a guest speaker, who had contracted HIV during college, share his experiences.

**Experience
Type: Extracurricular/Hobbies/Avocations
Experience Name: Treasurer, Pre-Medical
Society Dates: 08/20XX – 05/20XX
Contact Name & Title: Advisor
Organization Name: Pre-Medical
Society, University
City / State / Country: United States of America**

Experience Description: I restored university recognition to the organization and maintained budgets. I created an organization constitution, which had not been updated in nearly a decade, attending weekly extracurricular activities board meetings and submitting a proposal to the University Student Activities Committee for official recognition. The proposal involved a presentation of the organization's mission, how it would contribute to the campus community as a whole, a list of events planned, and submission of a sample budget. Following presentation of the proposal, the university officially recognized Pre-Medical Society. I spent the following two years at University as the organization's president.

Experience Type: Research/Lab
Experience Name: Summer Undergraduate
Research Program Dates: 05/20XX – 08/20XX
Contact Name & Title: Professor
Organization Name: Orthopaedics
City / State / Country: United States of America

Experience Description: I examined bone repair processes in rats as a function of age, prepared ulnae cross sections for microscopy, presented data weekly, and attended seminars on healthcare disparities and research development. We applied repetitive stress to the ulnae of young and old rats, inducing small fractures similar to those caused by repetitive activities such as walking. Using microscopy, we examined the extent of repair in each rat's ulna. Though we couldn't determine a mechanism to account for differences in repair, we concluded that repair processes are more efficient in younger rats and that small fractures are less likely to accumulate into a larger fracture in younger rats than in older rats.

Experience Type: Teaching/Tutoring
Experience Name: Tutor & SAT Coach
Dates: 08/20XX – 08/20XX
Contact Name & Title: The Director
Organization Name: Tutor
City / State / Country: United States of America

Experience Description: I assisted students in science, mathematics, Spanish, and SAT preparation. My clients included residents of The House, a juvenile halfway house for girls. They often had criminal records and were disowned by their families. I started out by helping the girls with general coursework and helped them develop effective study habits. My last summer at The House was devoted to SAT preparation. Because the girls required such individualized attention, I was able to tutor only one at a time. I borrowed from my experience as a catechist at St. Church by using individualized input for better understanding.

Experience
Type: Extracurricular/Hobbies/Avocations
Experience Name: Committee
Member, Orientation Committee
Dates: 08/20XX – 09/20XX
Contact Name & Title: Advisor
Organization Name: University
City / State / Country: United States of America

Experience Description: I helped incoming students transition to college life, communicated with students and their parents during the spring and summer before college, advised students on scheduling classes, and answered questions about campus life and university procedures. I was often assigned pre-health students and prospective science majors. The committee comprised about 30 upper classmen who were chosen from a pool of more than 100 applicants. Those interested in participating on the committee submitted a letter of intent and academic records to the University Student Activities Office. Applicants also underwent interviews with previous committee members and advisors.

Experience
Type: Extracurricular/Hobbies/Avocations
Experience Name: Project Member, Global
Project Dates: 08/20XX – 05/20XX
Contact Name & Title: Project Leader
Organization Name: The Project
City / State / Country: United States of America

Experience Description: I helped raise about $25,000 for travel and equipment expenses for volunteer work at boys' orphanages in Central America. I assisted the boys with chores, repainted buildings, and helped dig foundations for future residence halls for orphans. I also helped train these orphans in skills that would help them earn a living. The orphanages were part of the system funded by The Church and differed from most orphanages in not allowing the boys to be adopted. Boys were required to attend classes and pass exams to avoid expulsion. Because I was one of the few Spanish speakers on the trip, residents of El City often approached me for advice and asked me about life in America.

Experience Type: Honors/Awards/Recognitions
Experience Name: Honors &
Awards Dates: 08/20XX
Contact Name & Title:
Organization Name:
City / State / Country: United States of America

Experience Description: Award (8/20XX): Endowed in 19XX by the estate of Mr. Generous. Awarded annually to entering first-year students with scholastic ability who will study the natural sciences. Biological Honor Society (2/20XX): National honor society for students majoring or minoring in the biologic sciences. Spanish Honor Society (2/20XX): National honor society for students majoring or minoring in Spanish.

*Examples of most meaningful experiences.

PERSONAL COMMENTS

They were learning the basics of carpentry and agriculture. The air was muggy and hot, but these young boys seemed unaffected, though I and my fellow college students sweated and often complained. As time passed, I started to have a greater appreciation for the challenges these boys faced. These orphans, whom I met and trained in rural Central America as a member of The Project, had little. They dreamed of using these basic skills to earn a living wage. Abandoned by their families, they knew this was their only opportunity to re-enter society as self-sufficient individuals. I stood by them in the fields and tutored them after class. And while I tried my best to instill in them a strong work ethic, it was the boys who instilled in me a desire to help those in need. They gave me a new perspective on my decision to become a doctor.

I don't know exactly when I decided to become a physician; I have had this goal for a long time. I grew up in the inner city of A City, and attended magnet schools. My family knew little about higher education, and I learned to seek out my own opportunities and advice. I attended The University with the goal of gaining admission to medical school. When I started college, I lacked the maturity to focus on academics and performed poorly. Then I traveled to Central America. Since I was one of the few students who spoke Spanish, many of the boys felt comfortable talking with me. They saw me as a role model.

The boys worked hard so that they could learn trades that would help them to be productive members of society. It was then I realized that my grandparents, who immigrated to the US so I would have access to greater opportunities, had done the same. I felt like I was wasting what they had sacrificed for me. When I returned to University in the fall, I made academics my priority and committed myself to learn more about medicine.

Through my major in neuroscience, I strengthened my understanding of how we perceive and experience life. In systems neurobiology, I learned the physiology of the nervous system. Teaching everything from basic neural circuits to complex sensory pathways, Professor X provided me with the knowledge necessary to conduct research in Parkinson's disease. My research focused on the ability of antioxidants to prevent the onset of Parkinson's, and while my project was only a pilot study at the time, Professor X encouraged me to present it at the National Research Conference. During my senior year, I developed the study into a formal research project, recruiting the help of professors of statistics and biochemistry.

Working at the School of Medicine reinforced my analytical skills. I spent my first summer in the department of orthopedics. There I worked with an MD/PhD student to study the mechanism of bone repair in aging rats. The research, which shed light on human bone repair processes, fascinated me. I spent my second summer in the department of emergency medicine, working with the department chair, Dr. Excellent. Through Dr. Excellent's mentorship, I participated in a retrospective study analyzing patient charts to determine the efficacy of D-dimer assays in predicting blood clots. The direct clinical relevance of my research strengthened my commitment and motivated my decision to seek out more clinical research opportunities.

A growing awareness of the role of human compassion in healing has also influenced my choice to pursue a career in medicine. It is something no animal model or cell culture can ever duplicate or rival. Working in clinical research has allowed me to see the selflessness of many physicians and patients and their mutual desire to help others. As a research study assistant in the department of surgery at The Medical Center, I educate and enroll patients in clinical trials. One such study examines the role of pre-operative substance administration in tumor progression. Patients enrolled in this study underwent six weeks of therapy before having the affected organ surgically excised. Regardless of whether the tumor had shrunk, patients agreed to surgical intervention to comply with study requirements. Observing how patients were willing to participate in this research to benefit others helped me understand the resiliency of the human spirit.

Working in clinical trials has enabled me to further explore my passion for science, while helping others. Through my undergraduate coursework and participation in volunteer groups I have had many opportunities to solidify my goal to become a physician. As I am working, I sometimes think about my second summer in Central America. I recall how one day, after turning countless rows of soil in scorching heat, one of the boys told me that I was a trabajador verdadero—a true worker. I paused as I realized the significance of this comment. While the boy may not have been able to articulate it, he knew I could identify with him. What the boy didn't know, however, was that had my grandparents not decided to immigrate to the US, I would not have the great privilege of seizing opportunities in this country and writing this essay today. I look forward to the next step of my education.

CHAPTER 25

MEET MELISSA: EXPERIENCE DESCRIPTIONS, MOST MEANINGFUL SUMMARIES, AND PERSONAL STATEMENT

Despite a 3.7 BCPM GPA and a 33 on the MCAT®, Melissa was not accepted to medical school the first two times she applied. Her failure to be accepted might be because of a lack of clinical experience, a late application submission, or poorly executed written application materials. After the two rejections, Melissa enrolled in a special master's program to demonstrate that she could perform well academically and to boost her confidence by reentering a formal academic setting. Below is Melissa's application and personal statement that helped her gain admission to medical school. She is currently enrolled in an excellent medical school in the United States.

EXPERIENCES

*Experience Type: Research/Lab
Experience Name: Pediatric Cardiology
Research **Dates:** 09/20XX – Until Present
Contact Name & Title: Pediatric
Cardiologists, Electrophysiologist

Organization Name: Hospital
City / State / Country: United States of America

Experience Description: I worked in a pediatric cardiology lab on a multicenter retrospective study of patients who have undergone Fontan operations. My responsibilities included reviewing charts of patients who had one of two different types of Fontan operations and collecting data of what, if any, complications occurred. I then had to summarize this data and worked with my principal investigator to draw conclusions.

Most Meaningful Experience Summary: In my position, I have learned about the challenges facing patients who are born with congenital heart diseases that leave them with only one functioning heart ventricle. Fontan operations are available in two forms: extracardiac conduits or lateral tunnels. The objective of both operations is to divert venous blood returning from the body away from the morphologic ventricle and connect it directly to the pulmonary artery. The arrangement leaves the functioning ventricle to pump blood out to the aorta. The objective of the study is to compare these two surgical approaches and determine which is less likely to result in post-operative arrhythmia, a common complication. Investigators will compare the information I collect with data from similar studies being conducted in hospitals nationwide. I have presented the results of our research in a poster at an undergraduate symposium. Surprisingly, the son of one of the coordinators of the event was born with hypoplastic right heart and died before Fontan operations were performed. This child's mother thanked me for my work, which made me aware of the rich rewards of endeavors that have far reaching benefits. This experience has informed my interest in research and pediatrics.

Experience Type: Community Service/
Volunteer – Medical/Clinical
Experience Name: Shadowing Cardiologists
Dates: 09/20XX – Until Present
Contact Name & Title: Pediatric
Cardiologists and Professor of Residents
Organization Name: Hospital
City / State / Country: United States of America

Experience Description: I chose to shadow pediatric
cardiologists to complement the work I did in research.
I shadowed Dr. Binny in his office and in the hospital.
I observed as he interviewed and examined patients
and read EKGs and also had the chance to shadow his
colleagues in neonatology and surgery.

Most Meaningful Experience Summary: This year I
am working with Dr. Binny, a pediatric cardiologist who
focuses on electrophysiology. While shadowing, I watch
operations and observe Dr. Binny in his medical practice
as he speaks with patients and teaches residents. I
also interact with his colleagues, specialists in other
areas—e.g. neonatology and surgery—and shadow
them as well. I am now familiar with different sounds
of murmurs and with reading EKGs. Dr. Binny and his
residents have embraced my motivation to learn, and
I am grateful that they teach me whenever possible. I
have also furthered my knowledge of pediatric cardiology
through my own independent study via PubMed. An even
more important aspect of this experience is observing Dr.
Binny's interactions with patients. His respect for others'
emotional state and his commitment to communicating
effectively with patients so they can make informed
decisions about their health motivates me to pursue
medicine and to treat my patients with the same level of
compassion.

*Experience Type: Community Service/
Volunteer – Medical/Clinical
Experience Name: Shadowing Pathologist
Dates: 08/20XX – 09/20XX
Contact Name & Title: Dr. Pathologist
Organization Name: General Hospital
City / State / Country: United States of America

Experience Description: I've always been intrigued by pathology, which is why I shadowed Dr. Smith. I attended morbidity and mortality conferences, watched organs being examined and their tissue placed onto slides, and listened as recently autopsied bodies were presented. I learned along with residents as they studied different tissue samples and forensics cases.

Most Meaningful Experience Summary: My experience shadowing Dr. Smith proved exciting because pathologic studies are full of intellectual challenges. When viewing small slides of tissues one deciphers the gender, type of organ, and diseases it represents. The forensic aspects of pathology are also challenging because one must analyze and decode entire crime scenes as well as the body of the deceased to determine cause of death. If called to testify to a court, a pathologist not only explains the cause of death but is also responsible for giving the deceased a voice. In one case, Dr. Smith explained that an obese woman who died in a car accident—caused by a construction rig landing on her car—suffocated when her breast tissue was compressed against her face on impact. This poor woman had a painful death. Through his thoughtful analysis, Dr. Smith was instrumental in bringing to justice those responsible for this terrible accident. I have realized through this experience the diverse roles that doctors play.

Experience Type: Community Service/
Volunteer – not Medical/Clinical
Experience Name: Chair of the Zoroastrian
Youth Group **Dates:** 10/20XX – 02/20XX
Contact Name & Title: President
of Board of Directors
Organization Name: Zoroastrian Center
City / State / Country: United States of America

Experience Description: The Zoroastrian Temple hosts several events a year to bring Zoroastrians together to strengthen the community. Since we are a small religion—our membership is only 2.4 million people worldwide—remaining strongly connected to the community is essential for the religion's survival. As a chair on the youth committee board, I help organize celebrations for holidays and volunteer activities. Our most recent activity has been volunteering at a nearby Lutheran church, which acts as a soup kitchen to feed the homeless. I helped organize and publicize this and other events. It has been rewarding not only to help the homeless but also to encourage younger Zoroastrians to remain socially conscious.

Experience Type: Honors/Awards/Recognitions
Experience Name: Scholarship
Recipient **Dates:** 06/20XX
Contact Name & Title: Board of Directors member
Organization Name: Scholarship
City / State / Country: United States of America

Experience Description: The scholarship is given by a Zoroastrian organization to Zoroastrian youths who serve as good role models for others in the community. The organization looks for individuals who embody exceptional leadership in academics, community service, and life in general. The award is presented to three individuals yearly as role models for Zoroastrian youth to follow. I was very proud to receive this award and strive daily to contribute to the community through altruistic and academic achievements.

Experience Type: Research/Lab
Experience Name: Research with Dr.
X **Dates:** 06/20XX – 12/20XX
Contact Name & Title: Professor
of Cognitive Science
Organization Name: Language and
Cognitive Science Research
City / State / Country: United States of America

Experience Description: Our lab attempted to detail the cerebral organization of language in unimpaired populations through the use of brain imaging techniques such as functional magnetic resonance imaging (fMRI) and evoked response potentials (ERP). The objective of the research was to use this information to develop exercises for aphasic patients that help them reestablish pathways for language expression and comprehension. I analyzed data from a previously abandoned project studying the semantics of language processing and helped a PhD candidate complete her project analyzing language analysis pathways. I learned how to conduct research projects independently and how to study brain waves using fMRI and ERP.

Experience Type: Community Service/
Volunteer – not Medical/Clinical
Experience Name: Mentoring
Dates: 01/20XX – 06/20XX
Contact Name & Title: Volunteer Director
Organization Name: Friends
City / State / Country: United States of America

Experience Description: I met regularly with Kirsten, a student at The Middle School, serving as a role model to help her cope with the difficulties of school and home. When we first began meeting she discussed only family difficulties. I asked Kirsten to express herself through writing poetry, a constructive outlet for her emotions when I am not around. Poetry writing and reading are now her main hobbies. Since our first encounters, Kirsten and I have built a very close relationship, and she is now able to manage family problems in a more constructive way. Through this experience I learned how my values can positively impact others. Once an average student, Kirsten is now an honors student.

Experience Type: Research/Lab
Experience Name: Independent Study in Neuroscience Lab **Dates:** 12/20XX – 04/20XX
Contact Name & Title: Professor
Organization Name: The Lab
City / State / Country: United States of America

Experience Description: I studied the limbic system's role in neuron connection formation. As one of the major cellular pathways controlling protein turnover in mammalian cells, the system is activated at or recruited to synapses in response to neuronal activity. Alzheimer's and Lewy body disease are common causes of dementia in elderly populations. In humans, many of these neurodegenerative diseases are characterized post-mortem by anatomical hallmarks within the brain tissues, such as neurofibrillary tangles, plaques, and Lewy bodies, which are visible by standard light microscopy. Observations of these inclusions, tangles, and neuritic plaques have indicated that they contain high concentrations of ubiquitin.

Experience Type: Teaching/Tutoring
Experience Name: Teaching Assistant for Lower Division Biology Course **Dates:** 09/20XX – 06/20XX
Contact Name & Title: Student Affairs
Organization Name: University
City / State / Country: United States of America

Experience Description: I was honored to be one of five students per class invited to act as a TA. I was employed for three quarters as a lower division biology TA. The position required me to attend biology 1, a course with about 200-300 students, grade exams, and teach the subject material to smaller classes of students on a weekly basis. I held additional office hours, where students could ask me questions. Teaching has improved my public speaking skills and has given me a better understanding of the biology subject matter. I was able to impart my knowledge and moral guidance to lower classmen. I also used my section to remind students that they are learning to gain expertise, and I enforced academic integrity.

**Experience
Type:** Extracurricular/Hobbies/Avocations
Experience Name: Volunteer Chair of Zoroastrian Club **Dates:** 09/20XX – 03/20XX
Contact Name & Title: President of Zoroastrian Club
Organization Name: Zoroastrian Club
City / State / Country: United States of America

Experience Description: This club was created to bring Zoroastrian youths closer together. The religion has two sects —Iranian Zoroastrians and Parsis. The Iran sect stayed in Iran during Arab persecutions, centuries ago, while the Parsis found a haven in India. The geographic separation also yields different customs and often causes segregation within the faith. The major objective of the club was to bring both groups together for common causes—mentoring young Zoroastrians, completing altruistic activities, and educating the campus about Persian history. As chair, I helped find and organize charitable activities.

Experience Type: Community Service/ Volunteer – not Medical/Clinical
Experience Name: Canvasser and Field Director **Dates:** 07/20XX – 08/20XX
Contact Name & Title: Project Director
Organization Name: Environment
City / State / Country: United States of America

Experience Description: EC is a branch of an advocacy group that aims to protect citizens against special interest groups and political corruption. EC works to put environmental legislation on ballots so the public has the opportunity to vote and pass environmental laws. I worked to protect the state's beaches from cruise ships, bottom trolling fisheries, and other threats. I approached people on foot, educating them about supported propositions and volunteered to take on more responsibility; I supervised other workers who were trying to attain public support for proposed legislation. As a result of our campaign, the governor of my state implemented a progressive approach to protect our beaches.

Experience Type: Extracurricular/Hobbies/Avocations
Experience Name: Publicity Chair for Pre-Health for the Deaf Club (PHDC) **Dates:** 01/20XX – 06/20XX
Contact Name & Title: Advisor
Organization Name: Pre-Health for the Deaf Club
City / State / Country: United States of America

Experience Description: PHDC was created with the objective of teaching pre-health majors about deaf culture. The deaf are notoriously averse to seeking healthcare because of communication barriers. By teaching the hearing population about proper etiquette when interacting with non-hearing populations (or their translators), the deaf will be more comfortable with healthcare providers. I organized symposiums where deaf nurses and physicians spoke about the issues they faced in working with colleagues with normal hearing. I helped plan events for the deaf community. These events focused on preventive health measures they could take, such as nutrition and safe sex classes. I have also learned simple sign language.

> **Experience Type:** Community Service/
> Volunteer – Medical/Clinical
> **Experience Name:** Hospital Volunteer
> **Dates:** 11/20XX – 01/20XX
> **Contact Name & Title:** Volunteer
> Department Director
> **Organization Name:** The Hospital
> **City / State / Country:** United States of America

Experience Description: My first clinical experience was in college shadowing physicians at The Hospital. The Hospital is an educational and research institute. I gained hands-on experience in a variety of hospital settings. I worked in the critical care unit, where I was exposed to both surgeries and death. I helped move patients and transfer blood work, and I learned while experienced physicians taught residents. I interacted with patients, watched many medical procedures and observed the interactions of the physicians with their patients. The experience fortified my desire to pursue medicine, as I saw how physicians bring ill patients relief with medication, respectful interaction, and informed treatments.

Experience Type: Honors/Awards/Recognitions
Experience Name: The National
Dean's List **Dates:** 01/20XX
Contact Name & Title:
Organization Name: The National Dean's List
City / State / Country: United States of America

Experience Description: This award is given to outstanding college students who have been recognized by their professors for their hard work. The National Dean's list awards students from universities across the nation and has become the largest, most-respected program in the nation for honoring exceptional college students. After being nominated by my professor, I was awarded this honor in the fall of my junior year. This award reinforced my desire to maintain academic excellence.

Experience Type: Honors/Awards/Recognitions
Experience Name: Honors Award **Dates:** 12/20XX
Contact Name & Title:
Organization Name:
City / State / Country: United States of America
Experience Description: This award is given to students who achieved a grade point average greater than 3.5 during the school quarter while taking a full class load.

*Examples of most meaningful experiences.

PERSONAL COMMENTS

"Melissa, your uncle is coming to pick you up. Your mother has been in a car accident." I was dazed. As a 4th grader, I saw my mother as strong and infallible. I assumed that the doctor would give her some medicine and she would come home. Staring at her in the hospital bed, I overheard the physicians tell my father that she might not survive. After spending much of that year at her hospital bedside, I began to comprehend that my mother was even stronger than I had once thought. Even before she was able to fully open her eyes she still managed to cheer up me and my sisters by responding to the question of how many kids she had—what the physician asked to test her memory—by replying that she had three daughters and one adopted son. Her adopted son was our poodle. With time, my mother slowly began to talk and eventually began walking. She surpassed everyone's expectations and is currently a practicing oncologist. Even though I was a young child, this experience made me realize that some day I wanted to care for others as the doctors had cared for my mother.

Doing research initially inspired me to pursue medicine as a career. My first research experience, an independent study course in neuroscience, taught me that significant discoveries in basic scientific research can take decades to achieve. However, I also realized that though understanding disease processes can take an enormous amount of time, the potential to improve clinical outcomes makes these endeavors well worth that investment. I am currently participating in cardiology research, studying the complications associated with two different surgical approaches to the same congenital defect. I have presented the data in a symposium, and the abstract will be published in a university journal. Participating in this project has been informative in many ways: I've learned about cardiac physiology, gained experience executing and publishing research, and learned the importance of experimentation in medicine. This experience has further solidified my desire to make research a part of my future career.

My clinical exposures have also motivated me to pursue medicine. During undergraduate school, I shadowed physicians at The Hospital in the critical care unit. The greatest lessons I learned were through observation of physician-patient interactions. On one occasion I watched a physician bump into his patient when exiting the elevator. This patient, a young woman who had both arms and legs amputated, lit up and energetically greeted the physician. Then, while they talked and others passed by, her face became saddened by the stares of strangers. For me, this one-minute exchange solidified the physician's role. Yes, physicians aim to improve the quality of a patient's life by performing cutting edge research, collaborating with other physicians and medical staff, and providing clinical care. More important, however, a physician must treat patients as individuals, respecting their uniqueness and providing emotional support.

People often assume that I want to be a doctor to follow in my mother's footsteps. I tell them firmly that I have learned from my mother to pursue a career I am passionate about and to stop at nothing to attain my goals. This will not be my first time applying to medical school. My lack of clinical experience and a late application were major impediments in the past, and I have made up for both of these deficiencies. Also, to further my knowledge, this coming year I will be enrolling in a special master's program. I'm certain that pursuing a career to which I am completely committed, after exploring many fields to find my passion, is worth the hard work of resubmitting applications. With experience in research, clinical exposures, and numerous community service activities, I have discovered that medicine will allow me to be everything I desire: a researcher, a leader, a mentor, and a healer.

CHAPTER 26

MEET MIKE: EXPERIENCE DESCRIPTIONS, MOST MEANINGFUL SUMMARIES, AND PERSONAL STATEMENT

Mike was an outstanding athlete at a Division 1 undergraduate college where he played a varsity sport. He had an interest in medicine as an undergraduate, but his athletic pursuits were his primary concern. He earned a BCPM GPA of 3.0 and an overall GPA of 3.2. Mike knew that his only hope of gaining admission to medical school was to get a great MCAT® score, which he did —a 39. It was essential that Mike compose his documents carefully to express why his GPA suffered, while highlighting his dedication to athletics and to medicine.

EXPERIENCE

*Experience Type: Community Service/
Volunteer – Medical/Clinical
Experience Name: Shadowing
Contact Name & Title:
Organization Name: City / State / Country:
Experience Description:
Dates: 6/20XX – present

Experience Description: I shadow emergency physicians five hours per week. I try to shadow during different times of the day to gain a full understanding of time-related situations. For example, at night few consultants are available so the emergency physicians cannot reach patients' doctors. I also offer a helping hand while shadowing by, for example, getting needed items and helping doctors complete simple tasks.

Most Meaningful Experience Summary: When I'm not working, I shadow physicians in the emergency department. This has given me more direct exposure to physicians' work with patients than my job in the department does. I can follow the whole treatment process, from triage to discharge, and it's taught me plenty that will help me as a medical student and as a doctor. In particular, watching physicians communicate with patients in the exam room has been eye-opening. I see how the doctors fine-tune their approach for each patient and how crucial that is for good patient outcomes. We see a wide variety of patients in the ER. Some arrive with a full medical history and a list of their current medications, while others are completely unprepared. Many patients are unable to provide good information on their own due to trauma, drugs, or dementia. I observe the doctors as they work with the information available to determine the most important factors in the patient's condition and to come up with a treatment plan. It's also given me more perspective on doctors' thought processes as they diagnose the patient, which helps me understand why they order certain tests and scans. That experience will be invaluable to me as I go through medical school and begin my career.

*Experience Type: Community Service/
Volunteer – Medical/Clinical
Experience Name: Global Health
Contact Name & Title:
Organization Name: City / State / Country:
Experience Description:
Dates: 6/20XX – 7/20XX

Experience Description: Global Medical provides health care for underserved individuals abroad. I wanted to gain some more hands-on clinical experience and also have an interest in different cultures and travel. As a volunteer on a trip to Guatemala, I helped doctors administer medicine, do simple procedures, and communicate with patients. This was an intense experience, which required volunteers to work six hours a day in the grueling heat.

Most Meaningful Experience Summary: I spent a summer in Guatemala to provide free medical care for impoverished communities around the country. All the students on the trip were personally responsible for examining and diagnosing patients under the supervision of US and local doctors. It was a true hands-on learning experience, and I developed skills that will help me as a medical student and as a doctor. I learned how to communicate with patients across cultural and language barriers, take a medical history, perform a basic physical exam, and diagnose and treat some conditions commonly found in that part of the world. I also learned some of the basics of drug administration, since we ran a small pharmacy to provide the necessary medications for our patients. Helping these patients made me aware of the importance of understanding a patient's culture and background. Whether I'm helping a recent immigrant in the ED who doesn't speak English or someone who has beliefs different from my own, I learned much in Guatemala that will help me throughout my future career in medicine.

> *Experience Type: Intercollegiate Athletics
> Experience Name: Varsity Baseball
> Contact Name & Title:
> Organization Name: City / State / Country:
> Experience Description:
> Dates: 9/20XX – 5/20XX

Experience Description: As a varsity baseball team member, I practiced year round. During the spring, our competitive season, we practiced five or six days a week for three or four hours at a time and then had games, usually on Saturdays, starting in late February. In the fall, our off season, we lifted weights three days a week all semester and had four weeks of practice in preparation for a fall tournament.

Most Meaningful Experience Summary: My dedication and persistence in playing for the club baseball team paid off. At the beginning of my sophomore year, I was able to join the varsity team. Since playing on the team was a year-long commitment, baseball became an important feature of my undergraduate years. As I matured, however, I realized I wanted a fulfilling career and one that would offer intellectual challenge. Because I devoted so much of my time to baseball in college, my grades suffered and I knew I hadn't reached my true potential. Once I realized that I had possibly ruined my chances of pursuing a career in medicine, I studied as hard as I could for my MCAT® to demonstrate I was capable of doing well. I regret not putting in my full effort academically and since graduating college have devoted the same level of effort that I put into playing varsity baseball toward my effort to learn more about medicine. This focus and discipline will also help me be a better medical student and physician.

> **Experience Type: Paid Employment – not military**
> **Experience Name: Hospital Job**
> **Contact Name & Title:**
> **Organization Name: City / State / Country:**
> **Experience Description:**
> **Dates: 6/20XX – present**

Experience Description: I work three days a week in the emergency department. My duties are primarily administrative, which has taught me the importance of support personnel in helping a hospital function. For the ED operations to run smoothly, nurses, doctors, and support staff all need to work together and do their jobs well. I realize that their time is spent doing administrative work, and I feel that my experience will help my performance as a student and as a physician. My greater understanding of a hospital's administrative structure, as well as of the different responsibilities and perspectives of various hospital staff members, will allow me to function more efficiently as a team player in that environment.

> **Experience Type: Paid Employment – not military**
> **Experience Name: Bartending**
> **Contact Name & Title:**
> **Organization Name: City / State / Country:**
> **Experience Description:**
> **Dates: 6/20XX – present**

Experience Description: I tend bar four or five nights a week at The Cool Spot. I make drinks, keep track of money, and clean the bar. The main skill I've acquired from bartending is how to do my job in the face of any distraction—an important skill for a future physician. On busy nights, people often yell at me constantly while I'm making drinks, trying to be the next one served. Occasionally, customers will even start insulting me and other employees. Keeping calm, staying focused, and not getting distracted or flustered by the commotion is crucial both in serving customers quickly and politely and in making order out of a chaotic situation.

Experience Type: Paid Employment – not military
Experience Name: Trendy Clothing Clerk
Contact Name & Title:
Organization Name: City / State / Country:
Experience Description:
Dates: 12/20XX – 1/20XX

Experience Description: I worked at a Trendy clothing store over winter break during my junior year of college. I was a sales associate and worked the floor, helping customers and selling clothes. While most of our customers were friendly and understanding, some were not, and the experience taught me how to deal with people who are unappreciative and demanding. I was insulted or yelled at more times than I care to remember. I learned the importance of customer service and how to calm people down and see things from their perspective. Having gained more clinical exposure this year, I have also realized the importance of customer service in the practice of medicine.

Experience Type: Research/Lab
Experience Name: Research Assistant
Contact Name & Title:
Organization Name: City / State / Country:
Experience Description:
Dates: 5/20XX – 8/20XX

Experience Description: I worked in a lab studying apoptosis under Dr. X the summer after my sophomore year and learned firsthand how a cell research lab works. I was responsible for keeping the lab running smoothly, which included cleaning glassware, ordering supplies, making solutions, or helping researchers with their experiments. I quickly learned that research was not something I wanted to pursue as a career. I enjoy working with people, and I felt isolated doing this work, which was too disconnected from patient care to be fulfilling. At the same time, it taught me why understanding basic research is important to being a doctor.

> **Experience Type: Intercollegiate Athletics**
> **Experience Name: Club Handball**
> **Contact Name & Title:**
> **Organization Name: City / State / Country:**
> **Experience Description:**
> **Dates: 9/20XX – 5/20XX**

Experience Description: When Coach Z contacted me to play handball, I had never heard of the game before, but in the spirit of adventure I decided to accept his invitation and ended up loving it. I played goalie and helped our team win the collegiate national championship. This experience reinforced my ideal of approaching every experience with an open mind, and to always be willing to think outside the box. It also taught me the importance of recovering from mistakes. In handball, the goalie is expected to save only about 40% of the shots on goal – which means that it is crucial for the goalie to mentally recover from getting scored on and to remain focused on the game.

Experience Type: Intercollegiate Athletics
Experience Name: Club Baseball
Contact Name & Title:
Organization Name: City / State / Country:
Experience Description:
Dates: 9/20XX – 5/20XX

Experience Description: During my freshman year, I played club baseball after I was cut from the varsity team in the fall. We practiced twice a week and had games every two weeks, playing other club teams from the Northeast. Although I dreamed of playing for the varsity squad, the year I spent as pitcher for the club team was invaluable. In addition to keeping my skills sharp for the next year's tryouts, the experience taught me to deal with failure. It was the first time I wasn't good enough at baseball to keep moving forward. If I hadn't learned to find the flaws in my game and tried to improve, I never would have made the varsity team the following year as a sophomore.

Experience Type: Paid Employment – not Military
Experience Name: Internship
Contact Name & Title: Organization Name:
City / State / Country:
Experience Description:
Dates:

Experience Description: I interned at the US State Department throughout college in its computer program development area. I had a wide variety of responsibilities, including performing administrative tasks, helping coworkers develop computer skills, and analyzing project proposals. This was my first real job, and it taught me responsibility and how to work well with others. A few of my coworkers were state employees, but most were outside contractors who were brought in only for short projects, so the ability to quickly learn and keep pace with a new group of people was essential to working efficiently. I also learned the importance of accurate record keeping.

*Examples of most meaningful experiences.

PERSONAL COMMENTS

Sweat was pouring down my face as I sat in the cinderblock shack that doubled as a makeshift medical clinic. Along with two other students, I'd been seeing patients for seven hours – we'd started early that morning. I was so red and sweaty that I looked as though I'd spent my day working out in a sauna. It was Guatemala, and I'd spent the last two weeks traveling through the country with a group called Global Medicine, which provided free medical care. We were a mix of about 20 college students and recent graduates from the US, an American doctor and his wife, a handful of Central American doctors, and local translators. On this day, we were back in Guatemala after a tour through the rural countryside, and even indoors the smog seemed thick enough to coat one's body with grime.

Our translator, Maria, brought in our next patient – a young, worried – looking man. After introducing ourselves, we asked why he'd come to the clinic. A flurry of Spanish escaped from his lips. He had a rash, which had been spreading for some time. He lifted his shirt to reveal a vast discoloration over much of his chest and abdomen. It looked like another fungal infection, something we'd seen a lot during our trip. Handing him the medicine, I explained what he needed to do and gave him a sweat-soaked slip of paper with instructions on it.

Guatemala didn't have pharmacies on every corner as we do in the United States so I couldn't instruct the patient to buy the cream over the counter. The patient thanked us profusely. I was dehydrated, hungry, and tired, and plenty of patients remained to be seen that afternoon. As I watched him walk away, I thought about how different this experience was from my undergraduate years.

I always planned to go into medicine, but my college career revolved around playing baseball. My days were filled with weight lifting early in the morning and practice in the afternoon. Classes were sandwiched in between. I was a student-athlete, but most of my focus was on the "athlete" side. My single-minded focus on baseball couldn't last forever, and the bubble popped the spring of my junior year. It was the middle of baseball season, and it was going well – we had a winning record and it looked like we were going to qualify for the NCAA tournament. Since the tournament extends into summer vacation, my teammates were discussing how it would affect their plans. To my shock, many of my classmates were talking about having important-sounding summer internships at big banks and major corporations. I realized then that I had been distracted by baseball and needed to start actively pursuing my interest in medicine.

I knew that my academic record wasn't up to par. The Bs that I had considered perfectly acceptable early in college were below the averages for all medical schools. To demonstrate what I was capable of, I needed to perform well on the MCAT®. I put the same amount of energy into my MCAT® review as I normally did for baseball and performed well. My single mindedness about baseball also meant that I did not have time to pursue medically related activities during college, and I began to channel my focus to broaden my understanding of medicine.

Working in the emergency department (ED) since I graduated from college has allowed me to learn about the day-to-day working life of doctors. I realize that doctors must be excellent educators so patients understand what is best for them. I am impressed by doctors' mental stamina, essential for staying sharp during long shifts, their ability to find novel and clever solutions to problems, and their ability to stay calm during high-stress events. Listening to the doctors discuss their cases is one of the highlights of my job – I'll often ask why they ordered a CAT scan instead of an x-ray, or what they are looking for on a chest x-ray for a patient with chest pain. I find these intellectual challenges appealing.

My job has taught me about more than just what doctors do; I've learned about the patient experience as well. I've watched as overjoyed patients received good news, I've seen frustrated patients storm off after waiting for hours to be seen, and I've seen scared families trying to put on a brave face for their loved ones. I have gained an appreciation of how difficult it is to be a patient, especially in the ED. Our patients are sick, in pain, and scared and are questioned about personal topics while being examined by total strangers.Then they often wait for hours to find out their fate. Being a patient in the ED can be a lonely and frightening experience. I understand the importance of taking into account how vulnerable patients are while they are being treated.

My job in the ED has given me a glimpse of my future career. Those eight and 12 hour days working at clinics in Guatemala didn't feel like work. They were interesting and intriguing and reignited my passion for medicine. I have transferred all of the energy I used to focus on baseball to my future career in medicine. I am excited for the next phase of my education to help me reach this goal.

*Examples of most meaningful experiences.

CHAPTER 27

MEET DAN:
EXPERIENCE DESCRIPTIONS, MOST MEANINGFUL SUMMARIES, AND PERSONAL STATEMENT

Dan is a nontraditional applicant with a former career in the Navy and as a pilot. Dan had to prove himself academically though his postbaccalaureate course work since his undergraduate career was less than stellar and he had an institutional action. However, Dan's genuine commitment to medicine, maturity, and compassionate demeanor made it clear that he was an exceptional applicant and he was accepted to medical school despite some "red flags."

EXPERIENCE

Experience Type: Paid Employment – not military
Experience Name: Express Jet
Contact Name & Title:
Organization Name: City / State / Country:
Experience Description:
Dates:

As an airline pilot, I memorized the systems of the Canadian Regional Jet (CRJ), the limitations associated with the airplane, the emergency procedures, and the regulations for the safe operation of a passenger aircraft. I applied my knowledge to the decision making process during all phases of flight and emergency situations. During pre-flight, I filed the flight plan; reviewed meteorological information and passenger loads; and checked aircraft systems to make sure the plane was safe for flight. Inflight, I operated the aircraft, communicated with air traffic control, and monitored in-flight data to maintain situational awareness, make vital decisions and react in a dynamic environment.

> * **Experience Type: Paid**
> **Employment – not military**
> **Experience Name: Scribe America**
> **Contact Name & Title:**
> **Organization Name: City / State / Country:**
> **Experience Description:**
> **Dates:**

I worked side by side with physicians as their assistant, backing them up throughout the day. I researched patient history and created and maintained medical records for 20-24 patients in a 12 hour shift. I documented the patient's story, the patient's disposition, the procedures performed, the results of laboratory studies, and other pertinent information in an electronic medical record. In addition, I documented consultations with specialists and physician re-examinations, and I notified the provider when important studies were completed.

Most Meaningful: I left my job as an airline pilot to start the job as a scribe. Although my job as an airline pilot had more stability, more long-term security, and slightly better pay, changing jobs was a fantastic decision. I was a part of a professional team and experienced the good and bad aspects of medicine. I observed codes, centerline placements, incisions and drainage procedures, chest tube insertions, intubations, and other procedures. Through observation, I learned the art of patient interviews and how doctors adapt their interviews to the level of patient cooperation. I notice physicians routinely changed their follow-up questions based on answers to previous questions. I enjoyed learning things like how the QRS complex is affected by axis deviation and how CBC differentials point the physician to diagnoses. I was surprised by the ethical dilemma doctors face when dealing with a known drug seeker. The hardest day I experienced involved the death of a 4-month-old. It happened early in the shift, and I had to use the ability to compartmentalize I learned as a pilot to be productive the rest of the day. I knew I wanted to become a physician before my experience as a scribe, but becoming a scribe proved to me I enjoy the day – to – day aspect of the job, the environment, the team, and the patient interaction.

Experience
Type: Extracurricular/Hobbies/Avocations
Experience Name: Alpha Epsilon Delta
Dates: 01/20XX – 06/20XX
Contact Name & Title:
Organization Name:
City / State / Country: United States of America

Alpha Epsilon Delta is a pre-professional honor society dedicated to encouraging and recognizing excellence in pre-health academics. During my tenure as president from 2012-2013, our main focus was recruitment. I suggested to the officers that we have a membership drive, and I used contacts with a non-profit organization to plan and organize the event. With my direction, the officers who worked with me executed an extremely successful event. We added more than 20 members that year, no small feat for a new honor society. Additionally, we set in motion plans for the next class of officers to raise funds and establish shadowing and mentoring networks with the local healthcare industry.

> * **Experience Type: Paid**
> **Employment – not military**
> **Experience Name: Health Service Incorporated**
> **Contact Name & Title:**
> **Organization Name: City / State / Country:**
> **Experience Description:**
> **Dates:**

During my internship from 2012 to 2013, I was responsible for three major projects. It is known that families of lower socioeconomic class are less likely than those who are better off to take advantage of available healthcare programs. For my first project, I coordinated partnerships between HSI and Head Start. I formed memorandums of agreements with Head Start to enroll students and their families into a health care home. To maximize efficiency and minimize costs, HSI began an initiative to form partnerships with ancillary care providers. My second project involved coordinating these partnerships between HSI and local providers. My final project involved administering patient satisfaction surveys.

Most Meaningful: I went back to college after my Navy career to complete the prerequisites for medical school. During this time, I was fortunate to serve as an intern to the CEO of Health Services, Inc. (HSI), a federally qualified health center. In addition to the projects the CEO assigned to me, he let me rotate through the primary care department, pediatrics, pediatric dentistry, radiology, and laboratory operations. This allowed me to see the challenges management faces as it provides care to patients. I also met people affected by the lack of access to healthcare, which brought home the urgency of solving the problems Americans face in accessing healthcare. While shadowing the primary care physicians, I learned how many HSI patients are battling chronic conditions that plague families living in poverty. Watching the pediatric dentist provide care to a screaming child was an eye opener for me. However, the most alarming issue I learned about was how rampant and insidious periodontal disease is in families living in poverty. It is imperative these families have access to healthcare because without it they will never have a chance to rise above poverty. My CEO taught me the importance of balancing the business of healthcare with providing complete access to patients; one can't be sacrificed for the other.

Experience Type: Community Service/ Volunteer – not Medical/Clinical Experience Description: Non Profit Leadership Alliance (NPLA) Contact Name: Mr. Smith Organization Name: City / State /Country Dates:

The NPLA exists to provide nonprofit organizations with a dedicated and prepared workforce. Auburn University Montgomery's NPLA planned, organized, and executed an annual pet-adopt-a-thon, as well as Christmas and Easter parties for underprivileged children. For each event, we raised funds, coordinated sponsors and participants, purchased supplies and materials, advertised, and set up and ran the events. The children, more than anything, wanted someone to play with for the day. Additionally, I was selected as a NextGen Leader, a program that selects individuals who demonstrate leadership in their community and academics, as well as a commitment to a career in the non-profit industry.

Experience Type: Paid Employment – military
Experience Name: Navy Reserves
Contact Name & Title:
Organization Name: City / State / Country:
Experience Description:
Dates:

As executive officer, I was second-in-command for a 30 person unit. I supervised training, handled discipline issues, and was the officer-in-charge for two operations covering three weeks. Through my leadership experience in the Navy, I learned that most discipline issues were a symptom of a challenge the sailor was facing. As assistant operations officer, I managed a $672,231 budget and orders for 57 personnel. As a NATO exercise planner, I worked side-by-side over the course of a year with fellow military members in NATO countries, planning a NATO exercise involving 17 nations. I quickly realized the social interaction in European cultures was just as important as accomplishing daily tasks.

Experience Type: Paid Employment – military
Experience Name: Afghanistan Advisor
Contact Name & Title:
Organization Name: City / State / Country:
Experience Description:
Dates:

During my training to be a combat advisor in Afghanistan, I trained for a variety of combat skills, including Afghan culture awareness and Combat Lifesaver. I mentored the Afghan Air Corps in flight scheduling, risk management, and safely operating in a joint airspace. I coordinated and scheduled a variety of flights, including medical evacuation flights. I worked closely with the Italian and Spanish military to synchronize our operations. I spent a lot of my time building personal relationships with Afghan personnel (having daily tea, for example), as well as Italian and Spanish personnel. This helped me gain their trust and an understanding of how and why they plan differently from us.

* **Experience Type: Paid Employment – military**
Experience Name: Navy Pilot
Contact Name & Title:
Organization Name: City / State / Country:
Experience Description:
Dates:

In addition to my duties as an airline pilot, I learned the systems of 24 weapons and the tactics required to effectively employ them. I spent most of my flight time in extreme maneuvering that required the highest level of skill and absolutely no room for error. As I developed as a pilot, I became a flight lead, responsible for managing a team of airplanes flying together. During my 10 years of service, I was an integrated test and evaluation pilot, a flight procedures standardization officer, an aviation safety officer, an assistant operations officer, a weapons and tactics training officer, and a maintenance officer.

Most Meaningful: I experienced my greatest growth during my 10½-year career as a naval officer. I joined the Navy as a young, immature college graduate and was immediately thrust into an environment that demanded nothing but hard work and performance. My passion drove me until I developed the discipline to give nothing but my best. As I continued in my career, I began to mature, which prepared me for leadership positions that I would soon undertake. I made some mistakes as a new leader, like making decisions without consulting my staff. However, my unrelenting desire to give my all to those working for me motivated my personnel, and their commitment helped us complete the deployment with the highest mission completion rate, despite having the oldest jets in the air wing. Their dedication and success were not just limited to the workday; none of my sailors got into trouble when we visited foreign ports, no small task. Although I was trained as a pilot, during the last half of my career I was exposed to jobs I never imagined, teaching me how to adapt and apply my skills to situations that appeared to be completely unrelated to my training. When I experienced failures and disappointments, I evaluated what went wrong and applied the lessons I learned to situations I encountered later in my career.

Experience Type: Paid Employment – not military
Experience Name: Navy Student Pilot
Contact Name & Title:
Organization Name: City / State / Country:
Experience Description:
Dates:

As a student pilot, I learned the systems of the T-34C, T-2C, and T-45C airplanes, the limitations associated with the airplanes and their engines, the emergency procedures, employment tactics, and regulations applicable to the safe operation of a tactical aircraft. In addition to knowing that information, I was tested and evaluated on my ability to apply my knowledge to the decision making process in all phases of flight and emergencies. I routinely operated these aircraft at low and high airspeeds and extreme flight attitudes I interpreted complex data to maintain situational awareness, make vital decisions in a dynamic environment, and exercise hand-eye coordination to react quickly.

Experience Type: Honors/Awards/Recognitions
Experience Name: Military Awards
Dates: 01/20XX
Contact Name & Title:
Organization Name:
City / State / Country:

During my military service, I was awarded the Navy Achievement Medal, the Navy Commendation Medal, and the Meritorious Service Medal (an award usually reserved for officers two ranks higher) for exceptionally high performance in my jobs. I was recognized for preparing two separate commands for unit wide flying inspections, and I built and managed the Afghanistan Nation Army Air Corps aviation department responsible for the western region. I was also recognized as a Carrier Air Wing 2 Top Pilot for performing in the top 10 percent of the air wing's pilots while deployed to sea. I'm very proud of these awards because they illustrate how I have matured since college.

Experience Type: Honors/Awards/Recognitions
Experience Name: Deans List
Dates: 01/20XX
Contact Name & Title:
Organization Name:
City / State / Country:

I am exceptionally proud that I was on the Dean's List for the spring 2012 semester. My favorite class at Auburn was organic chemistry, specifically learning how to push electrons in reactions. I thoroughly enjoyed memorizing the rules and learning how to apply them to unique problems. During the summer after my Biology 1 and 2 courses, I took a biology class in Costa Rica, where I experienced the textbook in real life. My performance during my postbaccalaureate work at Auburn University is one of the proudest achievements of my life.

Experience Type: Paid Employment – military
Experience Name: Military Medical Trainiing
Contact Name & Title:
Organization Name: City / State / Country:
Experience Description:
Dates:

My military training involved studying physiology in basic aerospace physiology, naval aviation water survival training, centrifuge training, first aid, aviation safety officer school, and hypoxia training, a skill we used constantly as Navy pilots flying at high altitudes. In addition, I was certified as a Combat Life Saver. I was trained to treat and stabilize combat injuries (blast injury, amputation, severe bleeding, penetrating chest injuries), and I learned simple airway management, IV therapy and placement, and medical evacuation techniques. A real confidence booster came the day of our final exam, in which I placed an IV.

Experience Type: Community Service/
Volunteer – Medical/Clinical
Experience Name: Humanitarian Response
Contact Name & Title:
Organization Name: City / State / Country:

Experience Description:
Dates: 6/20XX – 7/20XX

On December 26, 2004, a tsunami hit Banda Aceh, Indonesia while I was relaxing in Hong Kong after spending two months on the aircraft carrier U.S.S. Abraham Lincoln. After boarding the ship and sailing to Banda Aceh, the carrier arrived on scene as the command post for disaster relief operations. There was little flying for a fighter pilot, but I supported the operations by coordinating flights ashore for medical personnel, medical supplies, food, and water. In my free time, I loaded water and rice onto the helicopters delivering supplies to shore. Even without meeting the people we helped, two miles off shore still on the carrier, I saw the disaster and knew we were making a difference.

Experience Type: Paid Employment – not military
Experience Name: Flying Instructor
Contact Name & Title:
Organization Name: City / State / Country:
Experience Description:
Dates:

I have nine years of experience as an instructor pilot. I taught subjects from basic aviation principles to advanced fighter tactics, including emergency training, flight by instruments, crew management, risk management, and aviation physiology. Every student is different, and I had to adapt my teaching style to each student and learn to present a topic using multiple methods. It's very rewarding to see students experience a sense of accomplishment once they grasp a concept or skill that has been eluding them. Every student has at least one maneuver they are uncomfortable with. I enjoyed working with them and watching them grow until they were comfortable with the maneuver.

Experience Type: Paid Employment – military
Experience Name: Military Deployment to Qatar
Contact Name & Title:
Organization Name: City / State / Country:
Experience Description:
Dates:

Currently, I am deployed with the Air Force to Qatar. I coordinate and schedule flights that support intelligence gathering missions. I have worked minimally with the U.S. Air Force in the past, and I am learning to understand and appreciate how they operate. Like most people and entities, they have their own goals, priorities, and challenges, and that dictates how they operate. This was an involuntary deployment, and, when I was notified of it, many people I worked with and know encouraged me to leave the Navy Reserves to focus on medical school. However, my dad taught me a commitment is not just for convenient times; you honor it all the time.

*Examples of most meaningful experiences.

Institutional Action

Because of immaturity, my first college experience resulted in poor performance. I was placed on academic warning the winter quarter of my freshman year and graduated with a less than average GPA. This performance does not reflect who I am now or what I am capable of today. Since that time, I graduated number one in my Navy primary flight training class and performed to very high standards in a very competitive career as a Navy fighter pilot. The 3.97 GPA I maintained in my prerequisite courses and studies while managing three part-time jobs represents my true academic abilities.

PERSONAL COMMENTS

My joints hurt, bubbles festered under my skin, and I worried I would never fly again. As I was treated for decompression sickness (DCS) from a scuba diving trip, I was fascinated by the technicians, nurses, and physicians working together, using technology to treat injuries ranging from DCS to diabetes. During my treatments, I considered the transition occurring in my life. In a few months, I planned to separate from the military and start a civilian life with my wife, and the DCS treatments at UCLA piqued my interest in the medical field. My conversations with doctors, medical school representatives, premedical school advisors, and my wife over the next year convinced me a career in medicine was the right decision. The technology, the team, and, most important, the opportunity to continue serving others inspired me to begin my journey in medicine.

I graduated high school in 19XX and began attending Outstanding University, planning to become a pilot. My father was a pilot and planted the seed of an interest that became an obsession. Unfortunately, due to my immaturity at the time, my college performance was subpar. Despite my grades, I was accepted into Navy flight training, igniting a passion I had never before experienced. I focused all my energy on learning to fly; as a result, I graduated number one in my class, flew the F-18 fighter jet, and ranked in the top 10 percent of fighter pilots on my aircraft carrier. My Navy career was a pivotal point in my life. I learned to study, work hard, apply discipline, and perform in a fast paced, high intensity, complex environment.

In August 20XX, I started my post-baccalaureate studies at Outstanding, while serving in the U.S. Navy Reserves, working as a flight instructor, being president of Alpha

Epsilon Delta, and serving as a Nonprofit Leadership Alliance NextGen Scholar. I enjoyed seeing how my life experiences related to science in the classroom. My background gave me a unique perspective, helping me learn new concepts. As a pilot, naturally I enjoyed physics, but my favorite class was organic chemistry. I knew it would be a challenge, but as the class progressed, I liked learning how organic chemistry relates to biological compounds and pharmaceuticals; it was the missing link in biology, explaining the "why" behind the "how" our bodies function.

While in school, I worked as an intern at Health Services Inc., a local health clinic devoted to providing access to health care regardless of income. As I observed physicians, I also saw the affliction caused by inadequate access to healthcare for those living in poverty. I witnessed three tooth extractions on children younger than 5 in one day of shadowing a pediatric dentist. The lack of health education and language barriers were as detrimental as the lack of health insurance, further illustrated by the lack of prenatal care for young, impoverished mothers.

In December 20XX, after completing my post-bac, I began working as an emergency room physician scribe. I learned two especially important lessons from this role. First, the physician's ability to earn a patient's trust heavily impacts the patient's outcome. For example, some physicians conducted their interviews in a collaborative manner, while other physicians' interviews were more like an interrogation. I noticed how a doctor's personality considerably affects the patient's interaction and cooperation; patients whose doctors sought to build rapport with them were far more likely to comply with their doctors' recommendations. Second, I thoroughly enjoyed the day-to-day work of a healthcare team. I learned to enjoy the successes and to understand the importance of strong compassion and acceptance for the inevitable sad endings. All patients deserve empathy and support, including those who have routine problems and simply need reassurance.

On the clinical side, I was also fortunate that some physicians taught me the basics of reading an EKG, an X-ray and a CT-scan, and how to interpret a CBC differential for differential diagnoses. The team environment was a major motivating factor for me at the beginning of my journey, and the scribe's job let me see it from a different perspective. As a scribe, I could watch codes and intubations from a slightly stepped-back position, allowing me to see everyone's role and how they individually worked in synchrony with mutual respect for each other. This type of teamwork was nothing like I experienced in the military, and it fueled the excitement I feel about medical school and a career as a physician.

My newfound interest in medical school surprised everyone I knew, except my wife. However, I believe things, including my decompression sickness, happen for a reason. As uncomfortable as it was, my illness ignited my passion for medicine. I was not ready for medical school when I graduated from college, but my Navy career was the right path to prepare me. Since then, my experiences at HSI and Scribe America have given me a more complete view of the social responsibilities and daily life of a physician. Now, as I prepare for medical school, I look forward with great zeal to my new adventure of learning and challenging myself as a physician.

CHAPTER 28

MEET MITCH:
OSTEOPATHIC PERSONAL STATEMENT

Mitch is a nontraditional applicant who applied to osteopathic medical schools. With a 22 and a 25 on the MCAT, Mitch needed to showcase how his former career and what he learned through his work made him an asset. He also needed to convey why osteopathic medicine was an ideal fit for him. Mitch does an excellent job illustrating his commitment to medicine and explaining why and how he made the well-informed decision to leave his former career to pursue medicine.

PERSONAL COMMENTS

Working as a police officer, one comes to expect the unexpected, but sometimes, when the unexpected happens, one can't help but be surprised. In November 2006, I had been a police officer for two years when my partner and I happened to be nearby when a man had a cardiac emergency in Einstein Bagels. Entering the restaurant, I was caught off guard by the lifeless figure on the floor, surrounded by spilled food. Time paused as my partner and I began performing CPR, and my heart raced as I watched color return to the man's pale face.

Luckily, paramedics arrived within minutes to transport him to a local hospital. Later, I watched as the family thanked the doctors who gave their loved one a renewed chance at life. That day, in the "unexpected," I confirmed that I wanted to become a physician, something that had attracted me since childhood.

I have always been enthralled by the science of medicine and eager to help those in need but, due to life events, my path to achieving this dream has been long. My journey began following high school when I joined the U.S. Army. I was immature and needed structure, and I knew the military was an opportunity to pursue my medical ambitions. I trained as a combat medic and requested work in an emergency room of an army hospital. At the hospital, I started IVs, ran EKGs, collected vital signs, and assisted with codes. I loved every minute as I was directly involved in patient care and observed physicians methodically investigating their patients' signs and symptoms until they reached a diagnosis. Even when dealing with difficult patients, the physicians I worked with maintained composure, showing patience and understanding while educating patients about their diseases. I observed physicians not only as clinicians but also as teachers. As a medic, I learned that I loved working with patients and being part of the healthcare team, and I gained an understanding of acute care and hospital operations.

Following my discharge in 2003, I transferred to an army reserve hospital and continued as a combat medic until 2009. Working as a medic at several hospitals and clinics in the area, I was exposed to osteopathic medicine and the whole body approach to patient care. I was influenced by the D.O.s' hands-on treatment and their use of manipulative medicine as a form of therapy. I learned that the body cannot function properly if there is dysfunction in the musculoskeletal system.

In 2004, I became a police officer to support myself as I finished my undergraduate degree and premed courses. While working the streets, I continued my patient care experiences by being the first to care for victims of gunshot wounds, stab wounds, car accidents, and other medical emergencies. In addition, I investigated many unknown causes of death with the medical examiner's office. I often found signs of drug and alcohol abuse and learned the dangers and power of addiction. In 2009, I finished my undergraduate degree in education and in 2012, I completed my premed courses.

Wanting to learn more about primary care medicine, in 2012 I volunteered at a community health clinic that treats underserved populations. Shadowing a family physician, I learned about the physical exam as I looked into ears and listened to the hearts and lungs of patients with her guidance. I paid close attention as she expressed the need for more PCPs and the important roles they play in preventing disease and reducing ER visits by treating and educating patients early in the disease process. This was evident as numerous patients were treated for high cholesterol, elevated blood pressure, and diabetes, all conditions that can be resolved or improved by lifestyle changes. I learned that these changes are not always easy for many in underserved populations as healthier food is often more expensive and sometimes money for prescriptions is not available. This experience opened my eyes to the challenges of being a physician in an underserved area.

The idea of disease prevention stayed with me as I thought about the man who needed CPR. Could early detection and education about heart disease have prevented his "unexpected" cardiac event? My experiences in health care and law enforcement have confirmed my desire to be an osteopathic physician and to treat the patients of the local area. I want to eliminate as many medical surprises as I can.

PART 6

SECONDARY APPLICATIONS/ESSAYS

CHAPTER 29

SECONDARY APPLICATION BASICS

After you submit your primary applications, schools will ask you to submit secondary applications (most automatically). Some of these secondary applications also require an essay and all require a fee! For each essay prompt you receive, pay attention to the character and word limits and use them as cues for how much information a medical school is seeking. A medical school that limits your responses to only 50 words, for example, is asking you for a simple, straightforward response. On the other hand, the school that allows 1,000 words per essay wants you to elaborate and go into some detail.

Secondary prompts vary, and I find that students can often recycle essays for multiple schools. But reading secondary prompts carefully is important. The most common mistake students make is providing a response that does not really address what is being asked. Even though writing secondary essays can get laborious, don't try to make an essay you have already written "fit" for a prompt if it just doesn't work. Remember, good secondary essays can help you earn a medical school interview.

Secondary essays that ask, "Why our school?" are always important. But if you composed an excellent primary application, other secondary essay topics may not be so important. Regardless, you should write every essay as if it is the only determinant of your success. Sometimes, especially if your primary application is comprehensive, responding to a secondary essay may force you to repeat information that is already in your primary application. That not only is okay but also suggests that you are in good shape; many schools determine prompts by identifying topics that applicants frequently leave out of primary applications.

I discourage applicants from writing a "one size fits all document" for various secondary essay themes (see "Common secondary essay themes"). Since the character/word limit for secondary essays is so variable (50 – 3,000 words) it would be a waste of time to write an essay before knowing specific character limits for each prompt. Having an idea of what you would write about for each of the common themes is wise, however. Some schools' secondary essay prompts do not vary from year to year, and you can often find these essay prompts and start working on them in advance. But, be warned, schools do change secondary essay prompts on occasion.

Common secondary essay themes

Describe Yourself/Autobiography
Provide Additional Information
Why Our School?
Personal Challenge/Moral Dilemma/Ethical Dilemma
Future Career
Personal Characteristics/Diversity
Describe an Important Experience
Describe a Research or Scholarly Project
What Are You Doing Next Year?

What Have You Done Since Graduating From College? (if applicable)
Optional Information

CHAPTER 30

EXAMPLES OF SECONDARY PROMPTS AND ESSAYS

Please write an autobiographical sketch.

This is my favorite secondary essay prompt as students can write these essays with ease because they don't feel restricted. Here is a good example of an essay written in response to this prompt; it includes some personal anecdotes and information that is interesting and that sheds light on the applicant's upbringing and interests:

I learned about the importance of dedication and commitment from my family. After my grandfather, Max, had a quadruple bypass when I was 12 years old, my sister and I would position ourselves on either side of him and take turns brushing his full head of fine grey hair. Never once throughout his medical stays or related complications did I hear him complain of any discomfort. Although he spent a significant amount of time in and out of hospitals due to congestive heart failure and stroke, Max's optimism and passion for life made him someone I always admired and strived to emulate.

Because of my evolving interest in medicine, my uncle, a cardiologist, invited me to shadow him at his office when I was a teenager. My grandfather's dedication to sustaining his own life was mirrored in my uncle's dedication to giving his patients the best care. But though I grew to admire this commitment, my cousins did not feel the same way because their father often missed their games and school events.

My uncle and my parents showed me the importance of committing oneself to a cause about which you are passionate. I espoused these values, dedicating myself to my passion for science and athletics. From elementary school throughout my sophomore year of high school, I competed in science fairs. My sophomore year of high school, my science teacher nominated me, along with four other students, to compete in the Big City County Science Fair. I took second place overall and advanced to compete in the Big State Science Fair for my project entitled "What is in Space?" This was when I started to gain confidence in my ability to excel in the sciences.

Though I played the flute in the school band from fifth grade throughout high school and performed as a ballet dancer, gymnastics, more than any other activity, truly tested my determination. I began competing when I was 7, often practicing five days a week. My academic performance still was my top priority, however, so I often woke up at 5am to complete my homework before going to school. When I wanted to take a day off, my mother reminded me that I had a commitment to my team. My skill at the gym nurtured my overall confidence in my abilities. My peers elected me team captain in 8th grade and again in my senior year of high school.

Another pivotal life experience was my own encounter with medicine. I vividly remember what the doctor said: "Once your scoliotic curve reaches 35 degrees, it will likely progress to at least 90 degrees." His words reverberated in my head like a ping-pong ball against a cement slab. The only 90-degree measurements I had previously come across in my 17 years of life concerned right triangles and the Pythagorean theorem, which were clearly not applicable at the time. Although I was extremely apprehensive about the needed surgery followed by wearing a back brace through the halls of my high school, I knew there was no alternative and consciously persuaded myself to think positively and see it as a challenge I would successfully overcome.

When I awoke from my surgery, I was determined to walk. Never had the pediatric orthopedic surgeon seen anyone standing on his or her own two feet so soon after a spinal procedure. I felt my valiant efforts had succeeded as I haphazardly plodded down the hallway with my IV pole lagging behind me. As a testament to this success, the doctor asked if he could refer other adolescents who would be undergoing surgery to me to discuss my positive attitude.

As I completed high school, my grandfather's prognosis grew grim. I decided to attend college in Big City so I could be close to my grandfather and spend more time with him. My childhood and adolescence helped me realize that I must work hard, persevere, and sometimes take risks to pursue my goals.

Why our school/optional information/additional information essay

Students who put forth outstanding primary applications may not have any new "optional" or "additional" information to address in an essay. In this case, consider responding to these prompts with a "why our school?" essay, an example of which is below. If you have had a meaningful experience or accomplishment since submitting your primary, however, you can use a prompt like this to describe that achievement:

My interest in geriatrics and emergency medicine evolved as I worked clinically in these two departments last summer. Through my course work in health policy, I also learned of the imminent need for geriatric specialized physicians to support the aging baby boomer generation. Through your hospital's renowned telemedicine and information technology departments, I would be offered the unique opportunity to explore this interest further. I would also take advantage of the medical school's summer research program to participate in research projects related to geriatrics or emergency medicine.

At the clinic where I worked, I gained firsthand exposure to disease complications, which often were caused by lack of access to primary care. My travels and work in India have shown me how common these issues also are internationally. Your unique medical school program would allow me to continue my active community participation during my first year, while providing care to diverse populations who lack access to care. This endeavor also could be augmented through participation in research and study in South America, so I could pursue my interest in global health while caring for other underserved communities and improving my language skills.

Of supreme importance, the urban location and suburban hospitals affiliated with the medical school as well as the Level I trauma center would offer unparalleled exposure to novel academic and clinical opportunities. Apart from the school's location in my favorite city of Great City, it is the superior curriculum, supportive medical educational environment, opportunity for community involvement, and team-oriented culture that would make your medical school a perfect fit for me.

Describe a personal challenge or moral or ethical dilemma.

Essays that ask about personal challenges or dilemmas are seeking information about your ability to manage conflict and challenge. Schools want to know that you make inherently ethical choices and can also consider all sides of a given situation:

I saw the Microsoft Word document on the screen of my roommate's computer. It looked familiar. I realized that this essay my roommate had written on the works and life of Jane Austen contained the exact language I had seen elsewhere. Where had I seen it? Why was this so familiar? I also asked myself, "Do I have a right to be looking at this document?"

Then it dawned on me. When my roommate got this assignment for her literature class, we discussed it with our housemates from down the hall. One girl offered to give my roommate a paper she had written on this topic for an AP class in high school. She printed out the paper and gave it to me to give to my roommate. Curious about the topic, since I am a Jane Austen fan, I read it before handing it to my roommate. The document on the computer in front of me contained parts of this paper that were copied, verbatim.

The issues here were complicated. First of all, I was invading my roommate's privacy. I should not have been looking at her computer even though we often shared our computers. But now that I was aware of what she had done, I felt an obligation to confront her.

That night, when my roommate returned home from studying, I first apologized for invading her privacy and explained that I had read the document on the screen. I then told her that I realized she had plagiarized and told her I thought this was wrong. She explained that she felt under tremendous pressure since she also had a big organic chemistry mid-term that week and it just seemed so easy to copy the paper even though she recognized it was not right to do so. With my urging, since she had not yet handed the paper in, she stayed up late into the night to compose an original essay and, in the end, she thanked me for noticing and for encouraging her to do the right thing.

How do you envision your future career?

You should answer this question honestly while trying to tailor your answer for each school. For example, a medical school that emphasizes research and scholarly achievement does not want to hear that you hope to practice only primary care. Such a school would want to know that you hope also to focus on research related to primary care, pursue a master's in public health, establish clinics for underserved populations, or practice academic medicine to motivate more students to follow in your path. If you have the room, you also might want to mention in essays like this how the school will help you achieve your goals:

I envision having a diverse career. I have enjoyed shadowing many different specialists and therefore am not sure of the specialty I will pursue, but right now I am curious about the practice of infectious diseases because of work on HIV research I have done at Best Medical Center. This research experience has helped me see that I can have a diverse career in medicine. My mentor, for example, cares for patients but also does research, trains residents, and goes on global health initiatives to help patients abroad. I see myself having an equally interesting and complex career because it will keep me intellectually engaged while allowing me to care for patients and teach tomorrow's doctors.

I am extremely interested in global health but have not yet had the opportunity to pursue it. In fact, one of the reasons I am especially interested in your medical school is because of its outstanding global health department and the opportunities for students to participate in projects internationally.

I see my future career combining my interests in clinical medicine, research, teaching, and global health and will likely pursue a career in academic medicine.

What personal characteristics do you possess that will add to the diversity of the medical school?

Medical schools have broadened their definition of diversity and for essays like this you can write about your unique interests, talents, or experiences. Or, you can also choose to write about your own experiences working with diverse populations:

I grew up in a diverse community even though my undergraduate college was quite homogeneous. During college, I sought out experiences beyond campus to immerse myself in more diverse communities. I volunteered in a free clinic, tutored children in Africa, and traveled during my vacations, when possible. I gained insights into the challenges facing others and how their backgrounds and experiences influenced their perspectives and attitudes. On a medical mission abroad the summer after my junior year, I worked in medical clinics helping to care for Mexican families, which helped me understand that such challenges and unfair inequalities in education and health care also exist internationally.

Through my experiences, I came to realize that all patients, regardless of their background, fare better when their unique circumstances, cultures, and outlooks are considered. To improve my ability to communicate with some of these populations, I minored in Spanish and became more proficient in the language through my studies in Spain. I have learned the importance of listening and seeing situations through the eyes of those I help. Throughout such experiences, apart from realizing that I hope to work with these populations as a future physician, I was continually reminded of the pervasive societal inequalities and injustices both locally and internationally.

What makes you special?

Essays that ask about your personal attributes give you an excuse to brag. Don't worry about sounding too "different" in these essays or "standing out." Schools want to know that you have the qualities and characteristics they are seeking. Before writing these essays, read the medical school's mission statement and review their student biographies (if offered) to get a sense of what the school values in applicants:

My Chicago college is located in one of the most diverse areas of the country, and living there for the past five years has afforded me numerous opportunities to help the surrounding community. I appreciated speaking with individuals living on Chicago Street outside the People's Mission throughout college, while I handed out food. This allowed me to understand that homelessness is often the result of circumstances beyond an individual's control. I also mentored students at the local elementary school, which gave me insight into the challenges facing these children and their families, most of whom were poor immigrants. Working with diverse populations has helped me understand the challenges others face. I thrive in these diverse environments and realize that all patients, regardless of their background, fare better when their unique circumstances, cultures and outlooks are considered.

To gain a better understanding of how to effect positive change from a policy standpoint, I enrolled in upper division health policy classes during college, an interest I hope to pursue in medical school. These diverse experiences along with my academic interests and coupled with my excitement for learning and my passion for exploration distinguish me from most other applicants.

Please write about a meaningful experience.

For an open ended essay, write about something that will make you stand out and about which you are especially proud. Medical schools want to know what types of experiences you consider valuable and why:

In college, I helped organize a research project studying malnutrition and offering basic health care in rural Indian villages. I spent months soliciting donations of medical supplies and medications and organizing volunteers and professionals. With a handful of undergraduate and graduate students and US physicians, and with the help of local government leaders, we created a makeshift medical clinic to provide care for more than 1,000 residents, some of whom trekked five hours to reach us. I encountered people my age who had never seen a doctor or a dentist. I also conducted surveys on what the villagers eat, and I am now summarizing that data and hope to return to India this summer to offer the villagers education on good nutrition.

This trip inspired me in many ways; I enrolled in Indian language classes to improve my ability to communicate and became more passionate about helping underserved populations internationally and domestically. I hope to work globally as a physician to help needy populations. I will also focus on helping underserved populations here in the United States. These experiences also inspired me to continue my research abroad to educate people, thus improving their overall health and putting them in control of their well being.

Write about a research or scholarly experience.

Several schools ask applicants to describe, in detail, a research project in which they have participated as an undergraduate. If you have the space, write about what you did in this research project, what you learned and how this knowledge will help your future career in medicine. As mentioned elsewhere in this book, the research does not need to be scientifically based; the skills you learned doing humanities or economics research, for example, can also be applied to medicine and science. Some schools will want to know details about your research while others want just a general overview; again, use the character count limits as an indicator of how much information they are seeking.

What are you doing next year or what have you done since graduating from college?

Answer these questions in a matter-of – fact way. Typically, medical schools require that only applicants who are not full-time students answer the question. In answering these questions, write about what you will be doing, but also include information about what you hope to learn and how this will prepare you for medical school.

For the upcoming academic year, I will continue my research on breast cancer at Outstanding Oncology Center, where I have been working for one year. Our findings last year have already provided evidence for the etiology of what receptor is involved in the development of tiny cell cancer, and we hope to build on these findings to continue our work. I have already become proficient in using the literature to design experiments, and I hope that this year I will learn how to analyze our findings. My hope is that our findings will be significant enough to lead to a publication on which I would be an author.

I will also shadow several doctors throughout the year to broaden my understanding of clinical medicine. Right now I have plans to shadow an internist, a surgeon, and an ophthalmologist.

My Saturday mornings will be spent volunteering at Inner City Clinic, where I will be promoted to the level of triage. I will be responsible for taking vital signs and basic intake histories on patients.

This year will be productive and, I hope, will provide the foundation I need to be an excellent medical student.

List your academic awards, health related experiences, research experiences, etc.

Respond to any essay prompt that asks for a list, such as this one, with a list. Do not embellish if an essay prompt specifically requests a list format.

PART 7

THE MEDICAL SCHOOL INTERVIEW

CHAPTER 31

INTERVIEW BASICS

If the medical school reviews your application favorably, it will offer you an interview (see "How do medical schools decide whom to invite and interview?"). At this stage of the admissions process, the outcome of your interview will be the most influential factor in your success. As already mentioned, subjectivity plays a large role in one-on-one interviews, which is why many medical schools are now adopting the multiple mini-interview and panel interviews.

The purpose of the interview is to evaluate your interest in medicine and if you have the qualities and characteristics we have described.

How do medical schools decide whom to invite and interview?

Every medical school has its own process for making decisions, but these are typical steps for the process:

Step 1: Application Screening: Most medical schools have cut-offs for GPAs and MCATs®; these criteria vary for each individual school. If your application doesn't meet these standards, the school won't consider your application further. If your application meets cut-off criteria, it will move to Step 2.

Step 2: Application Review: At least one individual reviews your application and decides if you should be offered an interview. That individual is usually a faculty member who will choose the order in which to review your materials. This is where a large element of subjectivity and reviewer style comes into play. One reviewer may decide to interview you after reviewing only your academic record, MCAT®, letters of reference, and briefly skimming your application, for example. Another reviewer might read every word of every application before making a decision. Some schools use "point" or "grading" systems to review applications. For example, they might assign points for grades, course selections, letters of reference, extracurricular involvement, outstanding accomplishments, written documents, etc. This is why your written documents must have broad appeal and tell a compelling story about your interest in medicine.

Step 3: Interview: If you are granted an interview based on the review of your application as described in Step 2, that interview will then be a major determinant of your success. Most medical schools conduct either one or two 30 minute interviews with faculty members or students. Just as a great deal of subjectivity plays a part in Step 2, even more subjectivity plays a role in the interview. More medical schools are now conducting multiple mini interviews (MMIs) and panel interviews, where several people evaluate each applicant so as to make decisions more objective and less influenced by bias.

Step 4: Applicant Presentation and Committee Vote: After your interview(s), your interviewer (or a designated individual if you had a panel, group, or MMI interview) typically will present your candidacy to all members of the admissions committee. A scoring system also may be in place, which also varies from school to school, and each interviewer may assign you a score, which he or she announces at the end of the narrative presentation of your candidacy. Everyone who met you on your interview day, both formally and informally, may also speak about your candidacy. After these presentations and discussions, a committee vote usually is taken to accept, wait list, or reject. Most schools have rolling admissions, while others release admissions decisions in March. Texas has a "match system," but Texas medical schools can also make "prematch offers."

Step 5: Admissions Decision: If you are accepted, you can hold a spot at more than one medical school until May 15th (April 30th for MD/PhD programs and April 15th for medical schools that start before July 30th), after which you are allowed to hold only one acceptance. If you are waitlisted, you must wait for the medical school's final decision. More about what can be done to get off a waitlist is found elsewhere in this book.

CHAPTER 32

INTERVIEW TYPES

The multiple mini interview

The MMI interview was originally developed in Canada and consists of eight or so "stations" through which each applicant rotates. At each station, you are given a scenario, are asked to role play, or may be asked to do a "team exercise" with another student. You are allowed a couple of minutes to read each exercise and must then have a discussion (lasting eight minutes) with the interviewers in the room (one to three evaluators per room) or perform the team task.

The scenarios are typically designed to evaluate your values and ethics and will present some kind of dilemma or situation to which you are asked to respond. Role playing exercises, during which you speak with an actor, test your communication skills. Team tasks are simple and again test your communication skills and ability to work with another individual. Some stations may be clinically based while others are not. Some medical schools' MMI interviews have no clinically based exercises.

The traditional interview

The one-on-one interview is still the most common, and it is important to approach each of them individually. Every medical school interviewer has his own unique style of interviewing to which the student should respond appropriately. For example, some interviewers have a standard list of questions that they ask all students while others prefer to have conversations. An interviewer's level of experience also influences her approach.

The group or panel interview

This type of interview typically consists of one to four students and two to four faculty members/current students.

I have written an entire book on the medical school interview, *The Medical School Interview*, which includes a description of various interviewers' styles and how to make the most of each type and style of interview, what to expect on interview day, and how to prepare. I highly recommend that you read the book—at least one month before starting interviewing.

CHAPTER 33

PREPARING FOR INTERVIEWS

It is important to practice interviewing by doing mock interviews. While no two interviews will ever be the same, practicing will help you become more comfortable speaking about yourself.

Before going to your interview, be aware of what aspect of your application and background you would like to discuss and try to bring up these topics during your interview.

Your interviewer's style

Many factors determine how your interview progresses, but the course of the traditional interview mainly depends on the interviewer's style, disposition, personality, and level of experience.

Know yourself

Interviewers are assessing your motivation to pursue a career in medicine, but they are also trying to obtain an idea of who you are, your values, your ideals, and your goals. This is why I encourage applicants to be aware of what distinguishes them from other applicants. Think carefully about the most important experiences in your life that brought you to that interview seat. Doing well on interviews requires that you be self-aware and able to express yourself articulately.

Know the medical school

Most medical schools will let you know, in advance, what type of interview to expect and how many interviews you will have. This information will help you prepare psychologically. Also be sure to research each medical school, in-depth, before your interview so you can intelligently express why you want to attend that institution.

Increasing your confidence

If you are lucky enough to have interviews at several schools, your confidence in your abilities will grow as the season progresses. However, almost everyone has at least one "bad interview" during this process when they didn't "click" with an interviewer, were asked off-the-wall questions, or had an interviewer who just wasn't in a good mood.

Interview follow up

If you have one-on-one interviews, be sure to send thank you notes or emails to your interviewer. This task is unrealistic if you have a panel interview or MMI, however, so instead send one thank you note to the director of dean of admissions at the medical school. I always recommend sending email thank you notes to interviewers instead of handwritten notes since this opens the possibility of dialogue between you and your interviewer.

PART 8

WHEN YOU ARE WAITLISTED

CHAPTER 34

WAITLIST BASICS

If you are waitlisted at a top choice school, you can influence your chance of being accepted off a wait list. Most schools will not reveal exactly how many applicants they "waitlist" (some are, literally, 400 people deep), but most will tell you what percentage of their class "comes off the waitlist." In general, more competitive schools take fewer people off the waitlist since at top schools, up to 75% of applicants who are accepted actually attend, compared with 35% at less competitive schools.

Most waitlists are non-rolling, and schools will consider waitlist applicants only after April 30th when all accepted students can hold only one acceptance (See "If I am accepted to another school, what happens if I get off a waitlist at a school I would rather attend?").

For medical schools that start classes before July 30th, however, you must hold only this acceptance as of April 15th (rather than May 15th). Some medical schools have "rolling waitlists" that are considered throughout the interview season. Some waitlists are ranked while others are not. Most schools will let you know their waitlist procedures if you are placed on their waitlist (See "Important dates for medical school applicants").

If I am accepted to another school, what happens if I get off a waitlist at a school I would rather attend?

You are allowed to accept a waitlist acceptance until you have matriculated in medical school. So, let's say you are accepted to medical school A, but really want to attend medical school B where you are waitlisted. If medical school B offers you a spot off the waitlist, you can withdraw from medical school A and attend medical school B as long as you have not yet matriculated at medical school A. What does matriculate mean? This means that you have already started classes, which usually start with orientation.

Important dates for medical school applicants

October 15 : Medical schools can extend acceptances after this date. The only acceptances that can be offered before October 15th are for early decision applicants.

March 15th: MD/PhD programs must extend a number of acceptances that is at least equal to the number of students in the matriculating class.

March 15th: Medical schools must extend a number of acceptances that is at least equal to the number of students in the matriculating class..

April 15th: Applicants who decide to attend medical schools that start classes before July 30th must withdraw other applications and commit to that medical school if they wish to attend. Applicants can remain on wait lists and can accept wait list offers before they matriculate.

April 30th: MD/PhD applicants can hold only one acceptance. Applicants can accept waitlist offers before they matriculate.

April 30th: Medical school applicants may hold only one acceptance to medical school. They can accept waitlist offers before they matriculate at the medical school where they are holding a spot. Before April 30th, students may hold multiple acceptances by submitting refundable deposits to medical schools.

After May 15th, schools may require students to respond to acceptance offers in less than two weeks. Before May 15th, students are allowed at least two weeks to respond to acceptance offers.

No medical school or program is allowed to extend an acceptance offer to a student once he or she has already started orientation or is enrolled in classes at another medical school.

CHAPTER 35

LETTERS OF INTENT WITH EXAMPLES

Sending a letter of intent to the top choice school where you are waitlisted is extremely important. Clearly express that the medical school is your #1 choice and that you will attend if accepted. You should also be specific about why you are interested in the medical school and try to relate those interests to your background and accomplishments. You should also update medical schools on any recent accomplishments. It also is wise to send additional letters of reference from professors or supervisors if this is an option. More support of your candidacy is always helpful.

Why are letters of intent important? Medical schools have several reasons for wanting to accept people whom they know will attend. First, medical schools want enthusiastic students who will add to the morale of the student body. They also like to know, especially as the date of matriculation nears, that the applicant they accept will attend; no medical school wants an open seat on the first day of classes. Finally, medical schools like the percentage of accepted applicants who matriculate to be as high as possible since this reflects the competitiveness of the medical school.

Sample Letters of intent

Letter of Intent #1

Dear Dr. XXX (Address this to the dean of admissions or the director of admissions, depending on the school's instructions):

I am a current applicant at The Awesome Medical School and interviewed there on October 25th. I am writing this letter to reiterate that AMC is my top choice for medical school and to update you on my accomplishments since my interview. If accepted, I would withdraw my other medical school applications and attend Awesome Medical School.

AMC will help me achieve my goal to one day become an excellent academic emergency physician. I hope to continue my research with Dr. Smart on the use of the novel new biomarker, C2D, for diagnosing a myocardial infarction. Dr. Smart currently is conducting this research in the emergency department. Additionally, since I have an avid interest in early goal-directed therapy because my grandmother died of sepsis and multiorgan failure two years ago, I look forward to working with intensive care physicians to learn more about this topic. With the many hospitals and free clinics that surround AMC, I will also be able to continue my work with helping the underserved. As a medical student, I will strive to be knowledgeable and compassionate and to make a meaningful contribution to the school.

Since my interview, I earned straight As in all my courses. I have also received a prestigious research award at my college. I have helped write a manuscript summarizing my research in the emergency department, which will be submitted for publication. I was named a Sherwood Scholar at my college because of the challenging workload I undertook and the grades I earned. I was also recognized by my peers through a Peer Achievement Award, which is awarded annually to two graduating seniors.

Thank you very much for considering my candidacy. I would be honored to attend AMC and hope to be accepted.

Sincerely,

A Future Medical Student

Letter of Intent #2

Dear Dr. Take Me,

I am writing this letter to update you on my accomplishments since I interviewed at Great School of Medicine in September. Since my interview, I have had interviews at several other medical schools and now know that Great is the perfect fit for me. If accepted to Great, I will attend.

As I discussed with Dr. Wish on my interview day, I have a commitment to help the underserved. I was impressed by the student run clinic at Great and was also intrigued by the number of faculty who are committed to helping the underserved. I feel that Great would provide me with role models who will help me develop into the type of doctor I hope to become.

I could also pursue my interest in neuroscience at Great. My undergraduate neuroscience research has been one of my most significant achievements as an undergraduate. Dr. Neuro, at Great, studies the same type of neurosynapses on which I have focused as an undergraduate. The neurology research together with the outstanding neurology department at Great would allow me to explore my interest in the specialty and establish my niche while still a medical student.

Finally, I really enjoyed meeting the current medical students on my interview day. They are bright, interesting, and supportive of each other. I can see myself fitting in very well at Great.

If accepted to Great, I will take advantage of the resources and opportunities available to me to hone the skills I need to become a great physician. I will work hard to become a valuable member of my medical school class and make a meaningful contribution.

Thank you for your consideration. If I am offered a position in the Great Medical School incoming class, I will enthusiastically accept it.

Best regards,

Aspiring Doctor

PART 9

DECIDING WHICH MEDICAL SCHOOL TO ATTEND

CHAPTER 36

DECIDING WHAT MEDICAL SCHOOL TO ATTEND

In making this decision, consider the same factors that were important in choosing where to apply, such as location, curriculum, cost, and graduates' success in the residency match (see Chapter 12). Talking with current students and recent graduates of the schools you are considering also is important; ask them if they think they are receiving a good medical education, if they are happy, what they do and don't like about the school, if the administration is supportive, and whether they are getting good clinical exposure.

Prospective students should also seek out information about elective rotations, which are taken during the third or fourth years and help you decide on a specialty. Ask how many elective rotations a school allows its students and when they can be completed; students who can take the most elective rotations and complete them as early as possible in the third and fourth years can apply early for residency. Many students complete elective "audition" rotations at programs where they are interested in doing residency and also obtain key letters of reference during these rotations. Since the residency application is due annually on September 1st (yes, you will have to complete another application soon!), you ideally want to complete these rotations before September.

If you are choosing between two or more schools, try to attend "second looks," which most medical schools host for accepted students in the spring before April 30th During second looks, you should seek out as much information as possible from current students and faculty. But keep in mind that these second looks are also recruitment efforts, and medical schools will be sure to put their best feet forward.

When do I have to decide where I will attend?

As of April 30th, you can hold only one acceptance. Until April 30th, you can hold multiple acceptances. As mentioned, you can attend a medical school where you get off a waitlist as long as you come off the list before you matriculate at another medical school.

PART 10

SPECIAL CONSIDERATIONS

CHAPTER 37

OTHER PROGRAMS

Postbaccalaureate programs

Many people decide after college or after pursuing a nonmedical career that they want to attend medical school, but they lack the medical school prerequisites. Most of the many outstanding postbaccalaureate programs are designed for such "career changers," but it is not necessary to enroll in one of these programs if you don't have the luxury of attending school full time or would prefer to take classes part time. Choose an extension program carefully, however. You want to attend one that has a good track record of getting people into medical school and is well respected by medical schools. However, full-time programs offer you the advantage of being with a peer group that is also working hard and a formal advising structure that can be helpful with the application process. Many of these programs are also well known and are respected by admission committees. If you take classes on a part – time basis, you may have less support and camaraderie. Regardless of whether you decide to enroll in a full-time program or not, I do recommend that you take all medical school prerequisites at a four year college rather than a two year or community college.

Combined undergraduate/MD programs

For high school students who are sure they want to become physicians, combined bachelor of science/arts and medicine programs can be an excellent choice (see "Medical schools with combined undergraduate/MD programs"). These programs are extremely competitive, and, in my experience, students who apply to them have often achieved as much academically and extracurricularly as traditional medical school applicants. Specific requirements for each program vary, but all require that students excel in the sciences. Most of these programs require that students apply both to the undergraduate institution and to the medical school affiliated with the program. Some of the undergraduate institutions use the common application and others have their own applications. The medical school affiliated with the undergraduate institution will also have a separate application. Programs vary in length from six to eight years.

When preparing combined program applications, students must consider what parts of the application will be considered for which parts of the program. Some medical schools will not view the common application, for example, and will consider only the medical school application, while other medical schools will read the undergraduate application and essays (or common application) and the medical school application. Making sure that you don't repeat yourself in the undergraduate and medical school applications therefore is important since both "pieces" may be reviewed by the same individuals. For many of the combined undergraduate/medical school programs, the undergraduate institution may not be especially competitive, while being accepted to the medical school is difficult. Usually the undergraduate institution accepts the applicant first and then recommends her to the medical school for consideration. Students then interview at the medical school.

For programs that are eight years, applicants should consider their decision carefully. Since most of the undergraduate institutions affiliated with these eight-year programs are not of as high a caliber as those where high school students with outstanding achievement might be accepted, many students decide to apply to undergraduate institutions and combined programs at the same time. If accepted at a high-level undergraduate college, these students will have the option of not compromising their undergraduate education and won't lengthen the overall time they spend in college and medical school. On the other hand, many students enjoy the security of knowing they already are accepted to medical school since they have a guaranteed spot (assuming they maintain a certain GPA) and often are not required to take the MCAT®, which can afford them more academic freedom as undergraduates. Refer to each individual program for specific requirements.

When admissions committees for accelerated programs review applications from such young students, they are looking for evidence of a genuine commitment to medicine, maturity, and the ability to manage a very rigorous course load. They want to be convinced that you aren't pursuing this path because it was what your parents wanted or because you thought it would be an easier path to medical school. Students in BS/BA-MD programs must maintain minimum GPAs, once admitted, and some must achieve a minimum MCAT® score to keep their spot in a medical school class. The school also wants to know that you won't be overwhelmed by the academics or that you will party too much without parental supervision.

Medical schools with combined undergraduate/MD programs

Alabama

University of Alabama/University of Alabama School of Medicine (8 years)
University of South Alabama/University of South Alabama College of Medicine (8 years)

California

University of California San Diego/University of California, San Diego, School of Medicine (8 years)
University of Southern California/Keck, School of Medicine (8 years)

Connecticut

University of Connecticut/University of Connecticut School of Medicine (8 years)
District of Columbia
George Washington University/George Washington University School of Medicine (7 years)
Howard University/Howard University College of Medicine (8 years)

Florida

University of Florida/University of Florida College of Medicine (7 years)
Miami University/Miller School of Medicine (7 or 8 years)

Illinois

Northwestern University/Feinberg School of Medicine (7 years)

University of Illinois at Chicago/University of Illinois at Chicago College of Medicine (7 years)

Massachusetts
Boston University/Boston University School of Medicine (7 or 8 years)
Michigan
Wayne State University/Wayne State University School of Medicine (8 years)

Missouri
Saint Louis University/Saint Louis School of Medicine (8 years)
University of Missouri-Kansas City College/UMKC School of Medicine (6 years)

New Jersey
Rutgers University/University of Medicine and Dentistry-New Jersey Medical School (7 or 8 years)
Rutgers University/Robert Wood Johnson Medical School (8 years)
University of Medicine and Dentistry-New Jersey Medical School (Has 7 year combined programs with eight New Jersey colleges)

New Mexico
University of New Mexico/University of New Mexico School of Medicine (8 years)

New York
Rensselaer Polytechnic Institute/Albany Medical College (7 years)
Sienna College/Albany Medical College (8 years)
Union College/Albany Medical College (8 years)
Brooklyn College/SUNY Downstate College of Medicine (8 years)
Stony Brook University/SUNY Stony Brook University School of Medicine (8 years)

Hobart and William Smith Colleges/SUNY Upstate Medical University (8 years)

St. Bonaventure University/George Washington University School of Medicine (8 years)

University of Rochester/University of Rochester School of Medicine (8 years)

Sophie Davis School of Biomedical Education at the City College of New York (7 years)

Ohio

Case Western Reserve University/Case Western Reserve School of Medicine (8 years)

Northeastern Ohio Universities College of Medicine (6 – 7 years)

Ohio State University/Ohio State University College of Medicine (7 years)

University of Cincinnati/University of Cincinnati College of Medicine (8 years)

Pennsylvania

Drexel University/Drexel University College of Medicine (7 years)

Villanova University/Drexel University College of Medicine (7 years)

Lehigh University/Drexel University College of Medicine (7 years)

Pennsylvania State University/Jefferson Medical College (6 years)

Rutgers University/Drexel University School of Medicine (8 years)

Temple University School of Medicine (8 years)

Wilkes University/SUNY Upstate Medical University (8 years)

Rhode Island

Brown University/Warren Alpert Medical School (8 years)

Tennessee

Fisk University/Meharry Medical College (7 years)

Texas

Rice University/Baylor College of Medicine (8 years)

University of Texas Pan American/University of Texas School of Medicine/San Antonio (7 years)

Virginia

Multiple Colleges/Eastern Virginia Medical School (8 years)

Virginian Commonwealth University/Virginia Commonwealth University School of Medicine (8 years)

MD/PhD programs

For applicants who have extensive backgrounds in research and who want to make research a major part of their future careers, combined MD/PhD programs are great options. Some students wrongly assume that being accepted by an MD/PhD program might be easier than obtaining admission to an MD program alone, but this is not the case. MD/PhD programs should not be considered "back doors" to medical school. Also keep in mind that if you are interested in research but don't want to invest the seven or eight years it will take to complete a combined program you also can participate in valuable research as a medical student, resident, or physician. Some students and residents even take a year away from their medical education or training to do a year of research and gain the skills they need to do research as attending physicians.

If you decide that an MD/PhD program is the best choice for you, you should be aware of several factors. Most

MD/PhD programs accept applications via AMCAS® and require you to write an additional personal statement about your research experience. Most MD/PhD programs accept current medical students from their own institutions who decide they want to pursue a PhD. Ideally, your research should be in depth and independent. Programs won't be convinced that you have a commitment to research if all you did was contribute to a project during one summer. Successful applicants most often have completed projects independently over several summers or during the course of a year or two. And don't think that your research experience excuses you from participating in other clinical and extracurricular experiences. MD/PhD applicants are expected to have the same level of involvement in these areas as regular MD applicants.

Some MD/PhD programs have their own admissions committees, while others will have two separate committees — one for the MD program and one for the PhD program. Therefore, interviews are typically conducted by MD/PhDs or by MDs and then PhDs who have a background in your research interests. When selecting programs, you should consider the strengths both of the medical school and of the basic science departments in which you are interested. At some schools, if you apply to the MD/PhD program, you may still be considered for the MD program alone if the PhD program doesn't accept you, but at other medical schools you may not be considered unless you are accepted to both programs. It is important to check each program's requirements and procedures when deciding where to apply.

A significant benefit of MD/PhD programs is that they are either fully or partially funded by institutions or grants sponsored by the National Institutes of Health for Medical Scientist Training Programs. Be sure to check with each institution for specifics about funding.

CHAPTER 38

NONTRADITIONAL APPLICANTS

Technically, any applicant who has taken one or more "gap years" between college and medical school is a nontraditional applicant. Based on AAMC® surveys of first year medical students, this category includes a lot of applicants, with about 50% of first year medical students taking at least one "gap year." With the increased number of medical school prerequisites, I anticipate that more and more students will wait at least one to two years after college to apply to medical school, and I doubt these students will be considered true nontraditional students. In fact, as mentioned elsewhere in this book, applicants with one to three years of added experiences often bring a greater maturity to the medical school admissions process and have more accomplishments and insights about which to write and discuss.

The true definition of a nontraditional student is likely to become one who is a "career changer," someone who has worked for several years, pursues post baccalaureate programs and then applies to medical school,. Career changers can add diversity to any incoming medical school class and often bring a unique perspective and level of maturity. At the same time, medical school admissions committees may be wary of people who demonstrate a lack of commitment and have had multiple careers or whose leadership positions in an earlier career suggest they would not fare well being in a subordinate position. Career changer nontraditional applicants should be aware of these concerns during interviews. All medical educators and clinicians have worked with career changers who had a difficult time returning to the classroom or with being "low person" on the totem pole and who underestimated the amount of work medical school would be. Some career changers have also felt, once starting medical school or even residency, that their former careers were more attractive than they had appreciated. I am not in any way discouraging this type of nontraditional applicant from applying to medical school; there are many successful career changers who become talented physicians. However, to do well in the medical school application process, a nontraditional applicant must be aware that medical schools might evaluate them with these considerations in mind. In both written documents and during interviews, career changers must clearly articulate why they left their former career, what appealed to them most about medicine to make such a drastic change, and what they have done to show a commitment to medicine.

CHAPTER 39

NEW MEDICAL SCHOOLS

Attending a new medical school can be an exciting prospect and offers unique opportunities. The leadership of new medical schools is usually energetic, optimistic, and excited to recruit its first classes of medical students. But you should consider several pros and cons when deciding whether or not to attend a new medical school.

First, the pluses of attending a newly founded medical school: Your classes probably will be small and you will receive more one-on-one attention than you would in a more established school. Medical school leadership will also be eager to make you happy and will likely listen to your concerns. Quite literally, your success, will reflect its success so it is in the medical school's best interest to teach you well and incorporate suggestions about what the school must do to improve. Some new medical schools are focusing on nurturing students who will pursue careers in primary care, and some are also hoping to train students who will remain in state to practice medicine. Keep this in mind when interviewing at new medical schools to make sure the school's mission and vision are aligned with your own.

A new medical school, like any new organization, will

likely have "kinks" it will need to work out. The process to become an accredited medical school in the United States is rigorous, and you will likely be paving the way for the medical students that follow you.

Here are some issues you probably want to address when deciding whether or not to attend a new medical school:

1. Who is the dean of the medical school and has he or she run other medical schools in the past? Someone who has successfully led another medical school will have vision and leadership skills that will likely contribute to the success of the new medical school, too.

2. How is the curriculum structured and, again, are the faculty experienced? You want to be sure that the individuals who will teach you are also experienced medical educators.

3. Where are clinical rotations? Most of your third and fourth years are spent in clinical settings so researching where these rotations will be completed is time well spent. Will you be doing rotations at an academic hospital that already has medical students? How will the hospital accommodate this increase in student volume? If no other students are working at the hospitals where you will be doing rotations, realize that your presence will also represent a culture change for that hospital; some will welcome your presence while others won't.

The medical school accreditation process

As you can imagine, becoming an accredited medical school in the United States is a lengthy and complex process. The Liaison Committee on Medical Education (LCME®) determines medical school accreditation. The LCME® has five distinct steps through which every medical school must progress to earn full accreditation:

Step 1: Applicant status

Step 2: Candidate school status

Step 3: Preliminary accreditation status

Step 4: Provisional accreditation status

Step 5: Full accreditation status

Medical schools can start interviewing applicants and enroll a charter class once they reach Step 3, preliminary accreditation status, but realize that it can take years to progress from Step 1 to Step 3.

For a full list of US medical schools and their accreditation status, see the LCME® website: www.lcme.org.

CHAPTER 40

FUNDING YOUR MEDICAL EDUCATION

The cost of medical school is overwhelming, but many options are available to pay for a medical education. In-state medical school tuitions average $25,000, and out of state and private school tuitions can be more than $60,000. With living expenses factored in, the annual cost to attend medical school can be up to $85,000!

Lenders consider the total cost of medical school (tuition, living expenses, transportation, supplies, books, and room and board) and subtract the student and family contribution to determine overall financial need. This calculation can be expressed by a simple equation:

Total cost minus all resources available to student (or expected family contribution) = Financial Need.

Even though some students have not depended on their parents for financial support for some time, the family is still considered the primary source of financing a medical education, which is why "family contribution" is factored into the equation. For federal loans, however, students are considered independent.

Be aware that once you are accepted to medical school you won't have to navigate the process of getting financial aid by yourself. Every medical school has a financial aid office, and most medical students graduate with some debt. Each medical school has specific procedures for applying for and receiving financial aid, something all students and their parents should know about. Here is a basic overview of funding options and process:

Federal loans are in two major categories

A   Unsubsidized loans. These loans are not based on financial need. They accrue interest once they are disbursed. Students are not required to pay interest if they are in school, during a grace period after graduation (6 months – 1 year), or when in deferment (based on eligibility).

B   Subsidized loans. These loans are based on financial need. They accrue interest only once the student completes school, has completed the grace period granted to recent graduates, and is not in deferment. Subsidized loans require submission of parental income tax information.

Names of common federal loans: Perkins, Stafford, Primary Care Loan, Graduate PLUS Loan. Each of the two types of loans has limits, which tend to be higher for unsubsidized loans.

Private loans

Private loans are offered by banks and typically have high interest rates. Medical schools may also offer loans to students.

Scholarships

Individual medical schools may offer students scholarships. Some medical schools have large endowments and may offer scholarships liberally while others have little scholarship money to offer. Medical schools offer scholarships after accepting the applicant. Scholarships do not have to be paid back. Private scholarships also are available; you can find out about them from financial aid officers at undergraduate and medical schools.

Grants

Some state and federal government grants are available to help students finance their medical educations. Grant awards do not have to be paid back.

Service commitment/loan repayment/forgiveness programs

In an effort to encourage medical school graduates to practice in underserved areas, usually in primary care, state and federal government programs have been designed to repay or forgive loans if graduates agree to practice in these areas for a certain period of time after training.

The US Army, Navy, and Air Force also have programs for students through which physicians serve in the branch that funded their medical education.

Applying for financial aid

Once you are accepted to medical school, you can apply

for financial aid. Processes vary for each school so you should consult the individual medical school. Here are the basic timeline and steps:

1. Complete medical school financial aid application and submit Free Application for Federal Student Aid (FAFSA): Every school requires that each student complete and submit the online FAFSA. This must be submitted annually in January. Parents' and the student's (if applicable) federal income tax returns should be filed as close to January 1st as possible since tax return information is required for financial aid applications. While FAFSA does not require that students include parents' financial information, most medical schools do require this information because medical schools factor family contributions into the scholarships and loans they offer. Based on a report generated by FAFSA, your school will then determine your financial need. Check with the medical school's financial aid office to ensure that this form is filled out properly; you must include the medical school's federal ID code to ensure that the medical school receives the report.

2. Consider loan options and complete applications: Meet with the medical school's financial aid officer to review the loans that are available to you. You may need to complete other loan applications (including private loan applications) in addition to the FAFSA. Many loan programs have limited funding, and if you apply too late you may not receive funding so apply for loans as early as possible.

3. Respond to award letter: Once you receive the medical school financial aid office's award letter

indicating what type and how much aid you are eligible for, respond quickly and decide which aid you want. These award letters are typically distributed every April 1st and on a rolling basis.

Newly admitted students receive financial aid applications after January 1st. You will not know the financial aid package a school will offer until your financial aid application has been submitted and processed. For many students, the financial aid package is an important factor in deciding which school to attend.

PART 11

REJECTION AND REAPPLICATION

CHAPTER 41

REASONS FOR REJECTION

If you were not accepted to medical school, you should objectively evaluate your candidacy to assess why you were not successful and to do what is necessary to enhance your candidacy. Medical schools rarely accept applicants who reapply without improving their candidacies and rectifying their deficiencies.

If you do not have any acceptances by January of the application year you need to start to carefully and thoughtfully strategize for reapplication. You don't want to come to the realization that you need to reapply in July or August, for example, and quickly submit a new application. You must reflect and seek out guidance on what you can do to improve. Your premed advisor or a professor can offer such advice. Medical schools that rejected you might also provide a "rejection analysis." The advice they offer may be superficial and useless, but sometimes this guidance is structured, direct, and extremely useful. You must also consider if you would like to improve your candidacy and reapply or whether you would consider attending an osteopathic or off-shore medical school.

The most common reasons that applicants are not accepted to medical school are as follows:

Poor academics/GPA/MCAT®

If your GPA is low, you must determine if this is what prevented you from gaining admission to medical school. Many applicants have poor academic records early in college and don't "blossom" until their junior or senior years or as postgraduates. You must show a convincing track record of academic excellence, and medical schools typically like to see at least two years of good grades in the sciences with a good MCAT® score. If you never blossomed as an undergraduate, you can still make up for your poor performance by repeating your undergraduate prerequisites, taking upper level science classes, or by enrolling in a special master's program.

If you think your MCAT® score may have prevented your admission, consider if a reexam might raise it. Most students who improve on a second or third MCAT® attempt can clearly identify what they did wrong on their first exam. If you did everything in your power to prepare for the MCAT® and nothing specific went wrong on test day itself, your score probably is a fair representation of your abilities and a retest won't result in much improvement. In this case, it is best to seek out feedback from medical schools at which you were rejected and find out if your MCAT® was the "deal breaker." MCATs® of 30 or above are rarely the "reason" that a student is not accepted to medical school.

Little or no clinically related experience

Many applicants who are not accepted don't have enough clinical exposure. Medical schools must be convinced that you understand what it means to practice medicine and that you have immersed yourself in clinically related experiences. Sometimes, depending on how deficient your clinical exposure is, all that may be necessary are some shadowing experiences. But if the last time you set foot in a medical setting was as candy striper in middle school, you will need to demonstrate significant effort to learn about clinical medicine. In this case, shadowing physicians, volunteering in a free clinic, and becoming involved in clinically related research will make up for this deficit.

Applied only to top-tier schools

Did you overestimate where you were competitive? Some students "aim high" without applying to any middle or third tier medical schools. Make a realistic evaluation of your candidacy and apply broadly the next time.

Poor interview skills

Interviewing is an art and talking about yourself isn't easy. Some applicants have the wrong impression of the interview; they think of it more as an interrogation than as a dialogue and enter interviews nervous and stiff. If you were uncomfortable throughout your interviews, it is likely that you need to work on your interview skills. I suggest seeking out guidance from your premed advisor or an expert in interviewing so you can practice and receive feedback on your interviewing skills. I also recommend reading my book, *The Medical School Interview*.

Poor letters of reference

Did you ask for letters of reference from people who knew you well and who supported your candidacy? Since applicants waive their right to read letters of reference, knowing if you have good letters of reference isn't always easy, but you can read the sections in this book on letters of reference to determine if you have the right "mix" of letters.

Poorly written documents

Some applicants take the wrong approach to their written documents, which serve as a screening tool for interview decisions. Did you write about your activities in a thoughtful and meaningful way? Did your personal statement highlight your most important experiences and communicate your interest in and understanding of medicine? Outstanding written documents are essential for all applicants but are especially important for applicants who don't have "perfect" MCATs® and GPAs. If you think poorly written documents are a significant component of your rejection, take extra care with them when you reapply.

PART 12

FINAL WORDS

I hope that reading this book has made it clear that while an applicant's "stats," such as GPA and MCAT® scores, are the most important factors in determining whether or not an applicant receives an interview, many medical schools "look beyond the numbers." Our goal has been to communicate that an applicant can do a great deal to influence his or her success in the medical school admissions process, an especially important message for applicants who don't have "over the top stats"— meaning most aspirants to medical school. In general, medical schools are placing more emphasis on evaluating applicants' "soft skills," such as communication, interpersonal abilities, and cultural awareness. Medical schools want to know that even the best applicants have those key qualities and characteristics we have listed here. Even if you know someone who "had the best scores ever and wasn't accepted to medical school," it doesn't mean that you will have the same fate because your scores were lower. An applicant's candidacy is multidimensional, and as you apply to medical school you should remember that each part of your candidacy is important.

Gaining acceptance to any medical school in the United States is a tremendous accomplishment and affords students the opportunity to care for patients. And, regardless of where you attend medical school in the United States, you can have the chance to practice the specialty of your choosing as long as you do the "right" things in medical school. But, I will need to write another book to address those concerns.

READ OTHER BOOKS BY DR. FREEDMAN

The Medical School Interview: From preparation to thank you notes: Empowering advice to help you succeed.

The Medical School Interview is a must read for every medical school applicant. Based on her experience as an admissions officer and as a private advisor with www.MedEdits.com, Dr. Jessica Freedman provides guidance on what to expect on interview day, how to influence what is discussed during your interview and what you can do to ensure a stellar interview performance. She also writes about what goes on "behind the scenes" after your interview and provides a transcript for a sample interview.

The Medical School Interview includes:

- What you must do to prepare
- What the interviewer is trying to assess
- How to influence the course of your interview
- The different types of interviewers and how this impacts your experience
- How you are evaluated
- What happens at the admission committee meeting after you leave *A sample interview with questions and answers.

The Residency Interview: How to make the best possible impression.

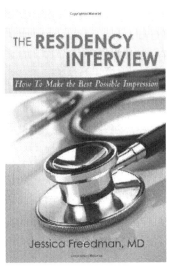

THE RESIDENCY INTERVIEW. These words make every applicant nervous. This MedEdits guide provides applicants with insight about the residency interview process as well as a general framework to dramatically improve their confidence on interview day. This book is based on Dr. Jessica Freedman's experience in residency admissions while on faculty at the Mount Sinai School of Medicine in New York City and her observations while privately advising residency applicants with MedEdits (www.MedEdits.com).

Get practical advice on:

- How to prepare for your interview

- What to expect on interview day

- The different types of interviewers

- What information you must convey during your interview

- How to structure your answers and direct your interview

- What to wear, how to behave on tours, lunches, "night before" gatherings and many other topics

ABOUT THE AUTHOR

Jessica Freedman, MD, was on faculty at The Mount Sinai School of Medicine in New York for nine years. At Mount Sinai, Dr. Freedman served in the residency leadership and on the medical school admissions committee and played a pivotal role in both resident and medical student education and curriculum development. Dr. Freedman has served as a mentor both formally and informally for countless residents and medical students, helping them to navigate the admissions maze. She has been working privately with applicants since leaving Mount Sinai in 2008 with www.MedEdits.com.

Dr. Freedman is the recipient of numerous honors. Her biography has been included in the Marquis Who's Who in America for the past five years and she has been quoted or published in the New York Times, Bloomberg, US News & World Report, Wall Street Journal, and Chicago Tribune. Dr. Freedman has professional writing and editing experience and has published extensively in the popular press, online and in peer-reviewed journals. She has published numerous articles on the Student Doctor Network. Dr. Freedman is currently a board-certified, practicing emergency physician. Dr. Freedman serves on the Medscape® Med Students advisory board and is a member of the Association of International Graduate Admissions Consultants.

Dr. Freedman received a nomination for the American Medical Association Women Physicians' Congress Mentorship Award, and was consistently evaluated a top faculty member by her medical students and residents at Mount Sinai. She is also recognized nationally as a leader in graduate and undergraduate medical education, served on several committees, including the National Council of Residency Directors, the Mentoring Women Task Force, Women in Academic Medicine Committee, the Medical Student Education Group and the Faculty Development Committee of the Society of Academic Emergency Medicine. Dr. Freedman is a graduate of Haverford College, Temple University School of Medicine, and the emergency medicine residency training program at Cook County Hospital in Chicago.

What is MedEdits, LLC?

MedEdits, LLC, founded by Dr. Jessica Freedman in 2008, is a medical education advising and editing company. Our company has two divisions:

1. Advising, interview preparation, and editing services by Dr. Jessica Freedman and our faculty, all of whom are former medical school or residency admissions members at well-known medical schools in the United States.

2. Editing by our small team of professional writers and editors. All documents submitted to MedEdits are reviewed by two professionals, a distinct

advantage over the single review offered by our competitors.

Dr. Freedman founded MedEdits, LLC based on the ideals she embraced while working in formal academic medicine. She considers MedEdits, LLC as the venue through which she can mentor and advise students and thus her roles are an extension of those she played in formal academic medicine. Many students and their parents work with MedEdits, LLC because they benefit from the advising and support they often feel is lacking at students' home schools. Other clients hire MedEdits, LLC because our editors provide additional support and editorial guidance. Unlike some other admissions consulting firms, MedEdits, LLC focuses solely on medical admissions.

Experience:

Dr. Freedman is the only private advisor who has served as both a medical school and residency admissions officer. She has been privately advising applicants since leaving the Mount Sinai School of Medicine faculty in New York in 2008. She thus has the unique perspective of understanding the medical education and admissions processes from both the "inside" and the "outside." She has also practiced medicine in a variety of settings, including competitive academic environments and community settings. All of MedEdits' faculty have a minimum of five years experience in academic medicine and working on admissions committees at leading medical institutions in the United States.

Ethical Standards:

The Association of American Medical Colleges® clearly states that it is the applicant's responsibility to submit materials that are composed entirely by the applicant. Realizing how important it is not to jeopardize an applicant's integrity, we edit documents with care and act as "essay tutors" to make suggestions for change but never compose a document for an applicant. In our editing, we ensure that documents are in the applicant's voice, writing style, and skill set since doing otherwise might influence an applicant's success. If an interviewer senses that you have not actually written your documents, he or she probably would mention these doubts in behind the scenes evaluations and, you would never know, for example, that your "great" documents actually contributed to that "waitlist" or "rejection" you received instead of an acceptance.

Comfort working with families:

We understand that many parents want to be peripherally involved in the admissions process and are comfortable partnering with them.

Results:

MedEdits has successfully helped hundreds of applicants through the medical school and residency admissions processes. Some are outstanding candidates while others are "borderline." We give every student individualized guidance based on his or her situation and background. Visit our website to see where our clients are accepted to medical school.

Up to date guidance and innovative solutions:

Dr. Freedman and the MedEdits team stay up to date with advances in medical education and admissions. We attend the annual Association of American Medical Colleges® meeting and read academic medicine journals. We are constantly trying to improve what we offer clients.

That our competitors often try to imitate what we provide is one indicator that we are leaders in the industry.

Professional editing that includes a "double read":

All documents submitted to MedEdits, LLC for editing are reviewed by two writing and editing professionals, all of whom have at least 10 years of experiences. This double read distinguishes us from the competition. Dr. Freedman trains all MedEdits editors in the art of medical admissions.

MEDEDITS MEDICAL ADMISSIONS

Hire a former medical admissions officer and professional writers to work with you.

What our clients are saying:

"I want to thank you for helping me truly express my experiences and intentions on my application to medical school. I feel that without the opportunity to work with you I may not have had any success. I am so grateful for all of your input and encouragement and perhaps we will work together again when I am applying for residency! The elusive dream that I have always wanted to pursue but had to build up the confidence for over the past few years has finally come true. Thank you again for all your help....

-Medical School Applicant, California

"I got into Cornell for medical school. YEAH!!! Thanks for all your help. The money I paid you was definitely worth it. It has made everything so much easier, thus avoiding any horrible acne outbreaks. Yay!...

-Medical School Applicant, New York

"It seems that [our daughter] has decided on Harvard for medical school. Your help to her has been truly invaluable and my husband and I both felt a tremendous sense of comfort in knowing that you were there to give [our daughter] such "spot on" advice and we could just hang

back and be parents through this very difficult and very very lengthy (seemingly endless) process...Once again, thank you again-you have been fantastic! Feel free to use us as references for other parents and I'm sure [our daughter] would be thrilled to be a reference as a student who has gone through the process. I'm sure she will be in touch before residency time!!!!! ...

-Parent of Medical School Applicant, Florida

"I appreciate the kindness you have shown to [our child]; I know it is a business, but I really do appreciate the nature of the advice and assistance you have given to her. You really have made [our child] feel like she has an ally in this ordeal – and for that, I am personally grateful to you...

-Parent of Medical School Applicant, New Jersey

"I believe it was all because of your step by step guidance and coaching/mentoring that you provided [my son] over the course of the year, on how to put his best foot forward in various situations that he has had success. He now has acceptances from a number of medical schools and will soon make his choice. I am very appreciative of your help for him during the process and thank you for all you did for him...Thanks in advance, and I hope [my son] will turn back to you when he is starting to think about residency programs etc. Once again, thank you so very much and let me know if there is anything I can do for you....

-Parent of Medical School Applicant, Michigan

"I got accepted to medical school! I definitely thought the interview preparation helped. At all schools I have been at I was noticeably less nervous than other applicants. I felt very confident and well-prepared thanks to your advice

and encouragement! Thanks so much for all of your help. As a reapplicant, I really think you took my application to the next level with your advice and expert editing team! Dr. Freedman and her editing team helped turn a decent application into an excellent one, greatly enhancing my AMCAS® entries, personal statement, and even providing help on secondaries....

-Medical School Applicant, Texas

"*We appreciate all the help you have given our son, a medical school reapplicant, during the application process. We definitely feel your guidance helped him immensely. Both my son and I feel that your intimate knowledge of the medical school admissions process gave us a thorough and sound advice throughout the entirety of the application cycle, from filling out the AMCAS® to interview day. We definitely feel your help strengthened the AMCAS® application and your interview feedback provided the confidence to perform well no matter the school. Working with you definitely improved my son's chances of acceptance. [Follow up: son will matriculate at a top US medical school.]...*

-Parent of Medical School Applicant, Illinois

RESOURCES*

American Association of College of Osteopathic Medicine®
(AACOMAS®):   http://www.aacom.org/about/Pages/
default.aspx.

Association of American Medical Colleges® (AAMC®):
www.aamc.org. The AAMC® represents accredited United
States and Canadian medical schools. At this site, you
can also purchase the book, Medical School Admission
Requirements, which is published annually.

Association of American Medical Colleges® Applicant,
Matriculant, and Enrollment Data: www.aamc.org/data/
facts. Use this data to see how you compare with other
applicants and matriculants.

American Medical College Application Service® (AMCAS®)
Applicant   Resources:https://www.aamc.org/students/
applying/amcas/181720/2012_applicant_resources.
html. Read the official AMCAS® instructions, course
classification guide, grade conversion guide and more.

American   Medical   College   Application   Service®
(AMCAS®):   https://www.aamc.org/students/applying/
amcas. Centralized application to apply to participating
medical schools in the United States.

American   Medical   College   Application   Service®
Letter   Writer   Application:https://services.aamc.org/
letterwriter. System through which letter writers can
upload letters directly to AMCAS®.

Free Application for Federal Student Aid (FAFSA®): http://www.fafsa.ed.gov/#

Medical College Admissions Test®: https://www.aamc.org/students/applying/mcat Through this portal, you can register for the MCAT®, find out about current fees, read MCAT® Essentials, access MCAT® practice tests and more.

Medical School Admissions Requirements®: Published annually, this must have resource is available in print and online versions: https://www.aamc.org/students/applying/requirements/msar/.

National Residency Matching Program® (NRMP®): www.nrmp.org. The "main" residency match. Site contains useful information and data about different specialty matches.

Texas Medical and Dental School Application Service®: http://www.utsystem.edu/tmdsas. Apply to Texas medical schools through this application.

*Some websites for these resources change annually.